THE SECOND PRINTING OF THE FIRST EDITION
OF THE OREGON OWNERS MANUAL IS DEDICATED TO
THE CITIZENS OF OREGON.

Working to preserve
this treasure called Oregon.

PO Box 1235
314 E Main, Suite 500
Hillsboro, OR 97123
1-800-333-SOLV (in Oregon)
www.solv.org

Copyright © 2002
ISBN - 0-9721618-0-5
Library of Congress Control Number: 2002107796
The SOLV Oregon Owner's Manual, 1st Edition
All rights reserved. Printed in USA.
Design: Sandstrom Design
Publishing Support: Graphic Arts Center Publishing®

Oregon Owner's Manual

—

PRODUCED BY SOLV
PHOTOGRAPHS BY RICK SCHAFER AND THE
RAY ATKESON IMAGE ARCHIVE

FIRST EDITION

TABLE OF CONTENTS

< MT. HOOD NATIONAL FOREST

ACKNOWLEDGEMENTS

FUNDING FOR this project was provided by the Frances A. Staten Fund of the Oregon Community Foundation and the Hannah B. Robertson Fund of the Oregon Community Foundation.

Oregon Owner's Manual sponsorship is provided by:

Maribeth W. Collins

Ron and Linda Klein

Heidi and Tony Leineweber

Mary Sampson and Robert DeGraff

Jack and Jan McGowan

Darcy and Mike Winslow

Special thanks go to members of the Advisory Group and statewide contacts who believed in the concept of the *Oregon Owner's Manual* and helped us shape the process for developing the piece.

Our heartfelt thanks to the "dream team" that helped us design and publish the *Oregon Owner's Manual*. They have long been partners in many SOLV projects and we appreciate their ongoing support and contributions: Sandstrom Design, Rick Schafer, the Ray Atkeson Image Archive, and Graphic Arts Center Publishing®.

Special thanks to Steve Sandstrom and Starlee Matz of Sandstrom Design who spent countless hours on the design of the *Oregon Owner's Manual*.

Many thanks to Borders Perrin Norrander, Revere Graphics Inc., and Moore Litho for production support.

Special thanks to researcher and writer Gordon Pennington and to IBM for contributing nearly two months of Gordon's time to the project. Thanks to volunteers Lee Hugill and Jolie Jordan. Thanks to Ron Klein and Metro Regional Parks and Greenspaces.

The *Oregon Owner's Manual* survey was designed by Amy Johnson of Lift Communications. Thank you. And thanks to all of the Oregonians who completed the survey and helped us shape the Oregon Practices section, or who wrote essays and other content for the *Oregon Owner's Manual*.

ADVISORY GROUP

Lois Achenbach, *Portland*

Gwyneth Gamble Booth, *Portland*

Marty Brantley, *Portland*

Mike Burton, *Executive Officer,*
Metro, Portland

Darrel Buttice, *Conkling Fiskum*
& McCormick, Inc., Portland

Sue Cameron, *Commissioner,*
Tillamook County

Gregory Chaillé, *President, Oregon*
Community Foundation, Portland

Kathleen Cornett, *Oregon*
Community Foundation, Portland

Janet Dodson, *Union County Visitor*
& Convention Bureau, LaGrande

Dennis Doherty, *Umatilla County*
Commissioner, Pendleton

Julie Ferreira, *Lake Oswego*

Andrew Fisher, *Rainier*

Melanie Florence, *Lakeview*
Revitalization Committee, Lakeview

Lorie Griffith, *Portland*

Ginger Harrison, *Portland*

Kathryn Harrison, *Tribal Council*
Chair, Confederated Tribes of
Grand Ronde

Larry Hilderbrand, *Editorial Board,*
The Oregonian, *Portland*

Andre Jackson, *Portland*

Betsy Johnson, *Transwestern*
Helicopters Inc., Scappoose

Chris McClave, *Portland*

Diedre Molander, *Oregon Business*
Council, Portland

Chet Orloff, *Portland*

Doug Pfeiffer, *Associate Publisher,*
Graphic Arts Center Publishing®,
Portland

Gary Reddick, *Executive CEO,*
Sienna Architecture Co., Portland

Karen Runkel, *Oregon Tourism*
Commission, Salem

Rick Schafer, *Rick Schafer*
Photography, Portland

Ethan Seltzer, *Director, Inst.*
of Portland Metro Studies-PSU,
Portland

Rev. Joe Smith, *St. James*
Lutheran Church, Portland

Bill Thorndike, *President,*
Medford Fabrication, Medford

Katy Tobie, *Community Affairs,*
Port of Portland, Portland

Jeff Tryens, *Oregon Progress*
Board, Salem

Rich Wandschneider, *Enterprise*

Duncan Wyse, *Director, Oregon*
Business Council, Portland

SOLV STAFF CONTRIBUTORS

Susan Abravanel
Angela Allison
Bev Ardueser
Sherry Britz
Claire Deremer

Cindy Dimock
Dan Enbysk
Debra Fife
Andrea Friedrichsen
Steve Kennett

Linda Klein
Jason McKain
Michelle Meyer
Pam Moreland
Jenny Peaslee

Erin Peters
Neil Schulman
Denise Smith
Nancy Spieler

YOU
ARE
HERE

OREGON OWNER'S MANUAL

—

A collection of contemporary and historic reflections, essays, and information about our beloved state.

Please read the *Oregon Owner's Manual* for a sense
of the abundance and variety offered by this beautiful
state, and to see why people love it. Turn to the Oregon
Practices on page 28 to see Oregonians'
suggestions on how we can keep it a treasure.

OREGON

BY BRENDA BURATTI, HILLSBORO

SHE IS the song I hear in the gusts in Ponderosa Pines, in the shrill call of coyotes in the night, in the perpetual rumble of the surf on sandy beaches, and in the crackle of glacial melt in the high country.

She is the scent of Cedar and Hemlock forests, the pungent rich earth of the valleys, the perfume of scarlet clover fields, and the salty brine of tide pools.

I feel her in the cool spray of her waterfalls, in the crisp air on the peaks of Mt. Hood and her Cascades sisters, in the sand on my feet at Cannon Beach, and in the summer rain against my skin.

She is the sight of soft white curves of the trillium in spring, the gnarled Junipers of the high desert—stalwart in the wind pummeled plain, the brilliant autumn yellow of Vine Maples in the Columbia Gorge, the painted hills and steep carved canyons of the east.

She is the taste of sockeye salmon, the sweetness of huckleberries, the crunch of hazelnuts, the succulent juice of golden currants, and the spicy essence of wild ginger.

She is the land that brings forth this abundance; for the first people who walked in deerskin moccasins and honored her spirit, for the pioneers in covered wagons who toiled six months to reach her, for the new travelers who arrive on blacktop freeways.

I hear the name we now call her in every drop of water that falls to nourish the soil, in every breeze that drives the clouds from the Pacific shores inland.

She has called me and I cherish her for these gifts.

She is the land I love.

She is Oregon.

INTRODUCTION

BY JACK AND JAN MCGOWAN
DIRECTORS, SOLV

THE PURPOSE of the *Oregon Owner's Manual* is to celebrate the places and the people that are unique to Oregon, and to remind us that we who have the privilege of living here also have the responsibility to take care of the land and of each other. Over the past two years, we've explored this theme and invited people from all over the state to contribute. The *Oregon Owner's Manual* is not the culmination of this effort but rather a step in a multi-genera-tion process that has inspired Oregonians to practice stewardship and be engaged in their communities every day.

Those who know us, have heard us describe the places in Oregon that we love and the people here who inspire us. We know Oregon as a treasure, inhabited by people who act to maintain a special quality of life.

During the summer of 2001, we had the opportunity to walk the entire Oregon coastline with our son Travis for the SOLV Oregon Legacy Walk. Step by step, day by day, broad sandy beach-es, craggy offshore monoliths, headlands dense with forest, and grassy capes were revealed to us. After 425 miles and 51 days, we could say without question that the Oregon coast is a spectacular treasure. As we walked, we met people who live on Oregon's edge, and others drawn to visit here. We had the time to hear their stories. And a common theme emerged. People love Oregon.

Oregonians are deeply connected to their place, and they care about what happens to Oregon. They share a sense of community and are willing to work together to ensure that Oregon remains the special place that it is.

For more than twenty years now, every summer for a week or two (and every other chance we get) we take off to wander around this amazing state. And we say amazing because we find ourselves awestruck again and again, year after year, by what we find during these trips. For us, Oregon's natural beauty and the

◄ SPECTACULAR ROCK FORMATIONS; LESLIE GULCH

people making their lives in her mountains and gorges, on her beaches and deserts, are what inspire us spiritually.

Tucked along a tiny stream in the Umatilla Mountains, we've camped for a week and looked out over miles of evergreens. Perhaps the view is broken by a lone gray snag. Beyond, to the east, the yellows and golds of the desert beckon. In Fossil, the last town before you head into these mountains from the west, there is one of those wonderful country stores. On the front porch you feel you've gone back a century. But inside they're talking about the latest software applications. We overhear the same conversations we're having back in our office in Hillsboro and, as if we were as well known here as we are there, people smile and nod as we pass.

Further south, we love the Ochoco National Forest, surrounding Big Summit Prairie in its center. These mountains are dotted with prairies and meadows. We have a favorite camping spot on the edge of a spring, where an antelope herd is likely to be seen about dusk. They share this particular spot with a rancher out of Prineville, who keeps his horses penned nearby. He's lived here since the '40s and says he knew as soon as he got here, like so many other Oregonians we've met, that this was the place he wanted to stay.

Out in the high desert are caves and bluffs. There are limestone columns and ornate pillars carved into hillsides by nature, fossil beds that speak of a time before humans arrived. Endless miles of sagebrush and juniper trees are broken by rivers (rivers!) and lakes. On a little lake in the far south of the state we camped one time, tying our tarps in the desert to the juniper trees to shade us from the sun that reached 106 degrees that day. We visited with the good people who owned the store at Plush.

To the east, Hart Mountain thrust straight up, towering over the lakes and marshes at her base. Up there we found petroglyphs, left by people thousands of years ago. Their stories too, tell of people enjoying the bounty and beauty of Oregon. Antelope and sunrises. Down into the Catlow Valley and then up again, to Steens Mountain, which plunges even more dramatically when you get to its eastern edge. Below is another lake, on the edge of the Alvord desert. We've camped there many times and experienced the wild wind as it raced around that grand drop.

Hot springs in the desert, people living in tiny towns and beautiful cities, views of mountains, of lakes and rivers, highways and dirt roads, wild bears and symphonies and museums and rain. Thunderstorms that shake the ground, rainbows that promise "things are different here." What has been different here, besides the stunning variety of natural beauty, is the independent, self-reliant nature of people. Perhaps it comes from being country settled by pioneers, perhaps from having such a small population in such a large area. Whatever the reasons, the strength of Oregonians to care for themselves has extended for generations to caring for their neighbors and their communities and has given Oregon a reputation as strong and independent as any of its residents.

In 1999, when *The Oregonian* published an opinion piece (please see page 25) which talked about the concept of the *Oregon Owner's Manual,* people responded from all over the state. The idea rang a bell. People told their stories, about feeling sad that the quality of life here is beginning to degrade. We heard about rudeness taking the place of kindness, traffic congestion and the resulting road rage, concerns about cigarette butts and fast food litter being tossed from car windows indiscriminately. And overall, people lamented the loss of a sense of community.

Many of the people who wrote and called knew SOLV as the statewide volunteer organization established by Governor Tom McCall in 1969. What they responded to with their hearts, was the idea of re-establishing the ethic described in a McCall quote. "Heroes are not giant statues framed against a red sky. They are people who say 'this is my community, and it's my responsibility to make it better.'"

Since its inception, SOLV has been a leader in volunteer community involvement. Today, it manages more than a dozen volunteer programs, from leadership training to on-the-ground projects. From beach cleanups to assisting senior citizens with their yard work, 90,000 volunteers currently participate in SOLV programs each year.

The *Oregon Owner's Manual* is our way of reminding all of us that Oregon is special and precious. As the generation with responsibility today, we must be diligent and take care that the special qualities of our place do not slip away, lamented but never to be recovered, once they are gone.

THE WORLD knows Oregon as a place of vast forests, tall mountains, and the majestic Pacific shore. In the minds of many, Oregon will forever be the land at the end of the Oregon Trail, a place of promise and new beginnings.

But Oregon is more than a place. In a real sense, Oregon is a state of mind, a way of living that places great value on the land, wildlife, and a culture of caring for one another. Oregonians take seriously their responsibility to manage their environment and their society. They give of their time and their personal resources to ensure that this place lives up to the promise that drove the pioneers to endure the hardship of the Oregon Trail.

Now more than ever we must renew our commitment to preserving those treasures that make Oregon special. Volunteer efforts by Oregonians are critical to achieving and maintaining a sustainable way of living—that is, a way of meeting our present needs that does not hinder the ability of future generations to do the same. Join the effort. Become a volunteer, and do something good for Oregon, whether helping SOLV keep the land clean and livable, or raising money to help the less fortunate. As William James said, "Act as if what you do makes a difference. It does."

JOHN KITZHABER, MD
GOVERNOR OF OREGON

◀ HIGHWAY 101 AT CAPE SEBASTIAN

COMMENTARY

OREGONIANS HISTORICALLY GO AGAINST THE GRAIN
—

An Oregon governor once told a President to go stuff his
Thanksgiving proclamation; independence continues

CHET ORLOFF
FORMER EXECUTIVE DIRECTOR OF THE OREGON HISTORICAL SOCIETY

JUST GETTING here, early Oregonians took the road less traveled.

The vast majority of those on the Oregon Trail in the
mid-19th century turned south to the California gold fields. A few
headed north, marking the beginning of the state of Oregon as we
know it now.

President Grover Cleveland issued his annual proclamation
declaring the last Thursday of November as the day of Thanksgiving.
Sylvester Pennoyer, governor of Oregon, in effect told the President
to shove off and mind his own business: "Oregon is ahead," reported
The Oregonian, as Pennoyer replied to Washington that Oregonians
would remember the Pilgrim's dinner on our own time. He promptly
declared November 23 as the day to celebrate.

We Oregonians are a contrary lot.

We've never outgrown the trait, fortunately for us and,
frankly, for the rest of the country. That certain nonconformity,
born in disparate geographies and bred in different societies,
stubbornly continues to influence much of what we do. It has
taken us in bold, but more often good directions.

It took years for many of the other states to catch up with
Oregon's initiative, referendum and recall governance. Today, for
all its many faults, the system is the stock in trade of participatory
democracy.

Governor Oswald West made the beaches open to all by
declaring the coastline a public highway and setting the course
for Oregon's 20th century conservation movement. What notions
in a land of private property! West dealt with legislators by
announcing that if they tried to kill off his measures, he would

"veto any bill that they fathered...whether it had merit or not." In 1911 he vetoed 63 bills.

The go-against-the-grain leadership of Wayne Morse (Vietnam), Maurine Neuberger (women's issues), Mark Hatfield (use of military force, health care and education), Tom McCall (land use) and Neil Goldschmidt (downtown revitalization) pushed and pulled Oregonians, and Americans, to think in new ways.

Consider Metro, still one of the nation's better efforts at regional government and yet one that few other regions have emulated—not from lack of trying and enthusiasm, but from lack of will and imagination. It will take decades even for many Oregonians to appreciate what future historians will acknowledge as yet another example of Oregon's being ahead of the curve.

Consider the vision of actually creating a regional city, connected by light-rail transit and supported by a regional growth boundary, within the tri-county area and Clark County, Washington. Some insiders grumble over why we do such things, outsiders come to Oregon to study how we do it in order to follow our lead.

We should also consider Oregon's questionable leadership in the Ku Klux Klan, one of the small number of missteps where the state misled the rest of the nation.

Moments of challenge seem to be needed to inspire us to follow the vision of our leaders: the social progressivism of the early 20th century, the political fervor of the '60s, the environmental activism of the early '70s, and the threat of destructive sprawl of the '80s. Such moments have come when Oregon has faced change or hard times. Historically, such times have generally called out exceptional inspiration rather than insidious desperation.

Faced now with international, national, and local pressures from the economy to education, it is time once more for Oregonians to do something exceptional. What do we have that, like any object held too closely, is difficult to see yet is uniquely ours, that we can steward in exceptionally nonconformist ways.

Oregon, in the words of its deeply missed laureate Terence O'Donnell, is a "time-deep land." The land itself and the history upon it are unique to Oregon. Considering all that we face today, how well we manage this land can continue to set us apart from, and put us ahead of, the crowd.

It has taken exceptional individuals and exceptional ideas to maintain what we have, and exception is a proud legacy. If we discard our gift of good land, nothing we do in the realms of education, engineering, or the economy will last long. If we keep this gift, future Oregonians will continue to appreciatively shake their heads at our contrary ways.

– EXCERPTED FROM *The Oregonian*, NOVEMBER 28, 2001

THE SPECIALNESS OF OREGON

BY TERENCE O'DONNELL

OREGON IS three places plus an ethos. It is the coast: a place of deep, impenetrable rain forests, bird-flocked estuaries, and high, surf-battered cliffs, a place fragrant with the smell of cedar, the rain-drenched firs, the salt of spray.

It is the interior valleys: the Willamette and its sister valleys to the south, the Willamette, with its meander of river, a vast green prairie swelling here and there into buttes, clustered with savannas of oak and containing some of the richest soil on earth.

It is the high country: snow peaks, distances and skies, and tingling, sage-scented air.

In all it is a ravishing panorama of extraordinary variety.

Then the ethos and the people who formed it. They came in the beginning because they sought a place bountiful, beautiful, and quiet. Wheat was not the only seed they planted. They planted too the seeds of certain values; the preciousness of nature, a distrust of bigness and immoderate ambition, cultivation over sophistication, the tendency to saunter rather than to run, all values confirmed over the years by newcomers who for the most part have come to Oregon because of the kind of place it is.

SOLV's call for essays stipulated that their subject be the specialness of Oregon. It is the essence of provincialism to think of one's place as special. And that's alright, for one of the virtues of provincialism is precisely that, to believe in the specialness of one's place and its values, for with that belief comes pride of place and with pride of place comes care of place and with care of place comes watchfulness. All is naught without watchfulness. Jefferson wrote that "Eternal vigilance is the price of liberty." It is also the price of a good place.

—

Terence O'Donnell passed away in March 2001 shortly after submitting this piece for the Oregon Owner's Manual. *Terence was a travel writer and lover of Oregon. His credits include inscriptions for the Vietnam War memorial in Portland;* The Garden of the Brave in War; An Arrow in the Earth: General Joel Palmer and the Indians of Oregon; Cannon Beach: a Place by the Sea; *and* That Balance So Rare: The Story of Oregon.

Governor Tom McCall with wife Audrey during an early beach cleanup.

EDITORIAL

AN URGENT CALL FOR REVIVING THE McCALL-ERA OREGON SPIRIT

—

Volunteers must rally to create the *Oregon Owner's Manual* aimed at reclaiming lost values

BY JACK MCGOWAN, EXECUTIVE DIRECTOR OF SOLV

THERE'S SOMETHING about Oregon. Some of us were drawn decades ago to this land of incredible and diverse natural beauty. Some, just unpacking the moving van, may still need to learn how to pronounce the name of the state, not to mention some of its beloved rivers and towns. But I have always believed that the only Oregonians who come here kicking and screaming are the ones who were born here. The rest of us came looking for a better life for ourselves and our children.

Besides our historical and geological uniqueness, Oregon's reputation for being slightly "behind the times" is considered an asset by many of its residents. We have escaped ugly metropolitan sprawl and boast the first landmark public-beach-use law in the continental United States. In fact, we have led the nation in many land-use and conservation efforts.

I am now in my 30th year as an Oregonian. For the past nine years, I have had the privilege of working for Oregon as the executive director of SOLV (formerly Stop Oregon Litter and Vandalism). Founded in 1969 by Gov. Tom McCall, SOLV ranks with such McCall legacies as the Oregon Beach Bill, the Bottle Bill, and land-use planning. McCall saw SOLV as an organization that would pay less attention to the political, social, and genera-tional things that might divide us, and more attention to the one thing that could unite us: a love for Oregon.

SOLV gives all Oregonians the opportunity to give some-thing back. We are at work throughout the state, on beach or illegal dumpsite cleanups, graffiti removal, wetland restoration, and hundreds of other activities, building community.

My work carries me across Oregon. When I talk to folks in such diverse places as Bly, North Powder, and Vernonia, I no longer hear their frustration with how the majority of economic prosperity has gone to the middle and upper Willamette Valley, or that Oregon's rush into the 21st century has overlooked them. Instead, I sense a concern that things are changing in Oregon, and not for the better.

This change manifests itself each day in the way our politics have become battlegrounds, not for the common good and vision for the future, but for limited personal views, regardless of how well-meaning they might be. Fading is the simple courtesy of letting someone merge in front of you as the morning commute unfolds. And look at the roadside litter. No matter how many times it's cleaned up, it returns with increasing frequency.

The opposite of vision is division. And I fear we are losing the vision that once united Oregonians. Waning is the profound respect for our land—the very spirit that propelled our earlier leaders such as Tom McCall, Wayne Morse, Edith Green, Ted Hallock, and Oswald West, among others. How have we lost that passion for preserving Oregon?

Let's reclaim that spirit by convening a group of creative, visionary Oregonians who will write the *Oregon Owner's Manual: A Guide to the Care and Feeding of the Oregon Spirit*. I think most Oregonians share my hunger for something to set a tone of unity and vision—something around which we can rally. If you love Oregon as I do, why not share your talents to ensure its future? Volunteer your time and energy to develop a guide for preserving the wealth we share.

We're looking for a few good Oregonians. You're probably one of them.

– PRINTED IN *The Oregonian*, AUGUST 29, 1999

THE NAME "OREGON"

HISTORIANS SAY Oregon was most likely named after one of two rivers. The Columbia River, which forms a coastline along the northern border, was at one time called the Oregon or Ouragan, which is French for hurricane. Others believe the name was derived from a mapmaker's error in the 1700s. The Wisconsin River was named the Ouisconsink and was picked up by travelers referring to the country west of the Great Lakes as Ourigan.

More knowledge of the origin of the word Oregon has surfaced in the last hundred years. Jonathan Carver may have appropriated the word, not the spelling, from Major Robert Rogers. Rogers used the form Ouragon or Ouregan in a petition for an exploring expedition into the country west of the Great Lakes. This took place in London in 1765. His petition was not granted. Jonathan Carver is the first person to use the form Oregon in referring to the river of the west that falls into the Pacific Ocean. This report was published in 1778.

Neither Vancouver (1778) nor Gray (1778) used the name Oregon by any spelling during their explorations. The name was not used by Lewis and Clark nor Astor's petition to Congress in 1812. Poet William Cullens Bryant, after reading a volume of Jonathan Carver's travels, mentioned Oregon in his poem "Thanatopsis" published in 1817. Pioneer travelers headed west to "Oregon, God's fertile land of plenty." So, however the name was derived or created, it stuck, and the Great Migration on the Oregon Trail had begun.

Source: www.webtrail.com

NEARLY 300 Oregonians took the time to complete the survey for the *Oregon Owner's Manual*. From a possible 72 options, they selected and ranked the 12 they thought most important to maintain Oregon's quality of life. (See survey, p. 34) By participating, they demonstrated how deeply they care about our state. What did they have to say? Here are the top 12 Oregon Practices. (Drum roll please!)

OREGON PRACTICES

Representing a cross section of Oregon

I.
Care for your health.
II.
Take responsibility for yourself.
III.
Reduce, reuse, recycle.
IV.
Conserve water, electricity, or other resources.
V.
Practice kindness, manners, and patience.
VI.
Make sure your guns are kept safely.
VII.
Get to know your neighbors.
VIII.
Use a less polluting product or method in your home,
yard, school, business, or community.
IX.
Vote.
X.
Keep your property neat and clean.
XI.
Dispose of litter and garbage responsibly; pick up debris.
XII.
Contribute to charitable causes.

A CLOSER LOOK AT THE
OREGON PRACTICES

THE ADVISORY Group and statewide contacts for the *Oregon Owner's Manual* spent considerable time thinking about the items that would go into the survey. Ultimately, 12 categories were established, with between three and 11 practices in each. All are practices that will contribute to the livability of Oregon. Looking more closely at the top 12 shows some interesting trends.

OREGONIANS ARE SELF-RELIANT

The top two practices, Care for your health and Take responsibility for yourself, are from the category Be Self-Reliant. Obviously, this is a trait important to Oregonians. We are known to be independent. We've been the first in the nation on many issues, from the Bottle Bill to land-use planning. Self-reliance gives us the strength and confidence to take a stand that may not always be in the mainstream.

Caring for our health and taking responsibility for ourselves are also important so that we can be strong to help others when they are in need. The outpouring of support shown by the "Oregon Flight for Freedom" for victims of the September 11, 2001 terrorist attacks in New York and Washington, D.C. came as no surprise to Oregonians. We see that kind of support here all the time. During the floods of '96, volunteers worked relentlessly, first to sandbag the streams and rivers rising over their banks and then for weeks afterwards to help property owners clean up. Recently, *The Oregonian* published a story about a community of farmers in Washington County coming together to plant the fields for a neighbor whose wife had been critically injured. In 12 hours they completed his two weeks worth of planting and pledged to be there to take care of the fields as long as needed. Then they returned to their own fields, to do their own day's work.

Oregon has long been a rural state and, over the years, the same kind of community caring took place during barn-raising parties, when self-reliant Oregonians got together to put up a new barn for a neighbor. Now, as then, we can't be in a position to help others unless we've taken care of ourselves first.

OREGONIANS CARE ABOUT THEIR ENVIRONMENT

Practices three, four, and eight are all from the category Live in a Sustainable Manner that Conserves Resources. The practices are Reduce, reuse, recycle; Conserve water, electricity, or other resources; and Use a less polluting product or method in your home, yard, school, business, or community. Practice 11, Dispose of your litter and garbage responsibly; pick up debris, is from the category Maintain and Improve Oregon's Health and Beauty.

These practices too, go back to Oregon's rural and pioneer history, when conserving materials and resources was important because of how limited and scarce they were. Oregonians are perhaps best known throughout the country for their efforts in environmental sustainability. From the nation's first bottle bill to land-use planning and recycling, Oregonians are leaders. True, we don't always agree and the issue of the environment can be a divisive one. But we understand the importance of conserving resources and caring for nature and believe it's the right thing to do.

We're also activists when it comes to sustaining Oregon's natural beauty. Each year SOLV involves Oregonians in approximately 90,000 volunteer positions, focused on keeping the state clean and beautiful and improving our waterways.

OREGONIANS ARE NEIGHBORLY

The categories of Be a Good Neighbor and Respect Your Fellow Oregonians, yielded three practices: number five, Practice kindness, manners, and patience; number seven, Get to know your neighbors; and number 10, Keep your property neat and clean.

Showing up all over the survey and being a catalyst for the *Oregon Owner's Manual* idea in the first place, being neighborly is perhaps one of the most important concepts behind keeping Oregon livable. No matter how beautiful the place we live, the experience of living here can be spoiled by interactions with people who don't practice neighborliness or are disrespectful.

"People are so much more rude than they used to be," has been a common theme in responses to the survey. Basic kindness, manners, and patience will go a long way towards restoring the sense of friendliness we are in danger of losing. After home and work, our neighborhood may be the place where we have the most impact on the experience of others. Why not make the effort to make that experience a little better by making sure we know who our neighbors are and that passing the place we live is a pleasant experience? Greet a passerby with a smile, good morning, or hello.

OREGONIANS' CARING EXTENDS PAST NEIGHBORHOODS

Oregon's current boundaries were established in 1859. With the creation of the state of Oregon, it's as if a magic line was drawn around the lands within. It's been said that Oregonians' pride for their state rivals that of Texans. There have always been issues that people in different parts of the state disagree on. Today we often hear about the rural—urban divide, a phenomenon certainly not unique to Oregon. But you also hear Oregonians lamenting this problem and seeking solutions. SOLV works in this arena, as do many state government agencies. The Oregon Community Foundation, the Community Oregon project of the American Leadership Forum, and others are all concerned about this issue.

Practice six, Make sure your guns are kept safely, was part of the category Promote Safety, but it also speaks to this concern for one another. We want Oregonians to be okay. Likewise, Practice 12, Contribute to charitable causes, from the category Give of Yourself and Your Resources, speaks to our concern for one another and our state.

We as Oregonians are learning to share our resources through donations to support the causes we believe in. We're just beginning to find out how much we can do, all around the state, by writing a check and volunteering through a non-profit organization. But Oregonians have always given generously. It might have been the meal prepared for someone who was ill, or the Christmas gifts left in secret for a family who couldn't afford them. Oregonians are charitable and we care deeply about each other.

OREGONIANS ARE ACTIVISTS

Oregon's motto, "She flies with her own wings," says a lot about how we view ourselves and our place in the world. We're not shy about taking the road less traveled or marching to a different drummer. And when we get a bee in our bonnet, we'll stand up for what we believe in.

The simple advice in practice number nine, Vote, comes from the category Be Engaged with Oregon Politics. Eighty percent of registered Oregon voters participated in the 2000 General Election. Nationally, Oregon ranked ninth in voter participation.

A RESPONSE TO THE QUESTION

"WHY IS OREGON SPECIAL AND WORTH PRESERVING?"

THE VOTERS' pamphlet is a unique aspect of Oregon politics and, by extension, of Oregon life. In the four states in which I have lived, the State of Oregon is the only state that has seemingly taken any responsibility to make me an informed voter through the distribution of the voters' pamphlet. I am not suggesting that it is necessarily the state's responsibility to educate voters, but for a casual follower of Oregon politics like myself, the voters' pamphlet provides me with comprehensive and well-organized access to the Measures and the candidates. In size, the pamphlet is formidable and grows larger every year, but what this growth suggests to me is that it wields considerable influence over voters, and therefore its place in Oregon politics is not insignificant. Without a doubt, many of the arguments in favor and in opposition of the Measures are redundant and sometimes irritating, but in the final analysis they are all in the spirit of open debate. Admittedly for me, the availability of the voters' pamphlet is the definitive difference between a thoughtful vote and a careless one. It is a personal challenge to me to take serious responsibility for my voting decisions.

— MELANIE K. MOLER, HILLSBORO

CAPE ARAGO LIGHTHOUSE
Coos County

OREGON PRACTICES SURVEY
—

What must we do to maintain Oregon's quality of life?
Here are the practices Oregonians chose from.

BE A GOOD NEIGHBOR
- ☐ Get to know your neighbors
- ☐ Keep pets quiet, under control, and manage their waste
- ☐ Watch out for neighborhood children; become a block home
- ☐ Welcome newcomers
- ☐ Participate in your neighborhood association
- ☐ Keep your property neat and clean

BE ENGAGED WITH OREGON POLITICS
- ☐ Learn about an issue that affects our state or your community
- ☐ Vote
- ☐ Discuss an issue with friends and co-workers
- ☐ Volunteer to register voters
- ☐ Learn about Oregon's land-use laws
- ☐ Choose an issue to support
- ☐ Volunteer for a government board, committee, or commission
- ☐ Work to change a bad law; don't just break it

BE SELF-RELIANT
- ☐ Care for your health
- ☐ Take responsibility for yourself
- ☐ Prepare for emergencies

LIVE IN A SUSTAINABLE MANNER THAT CONSERVES RESOURCES
- ☐ Be economical or thrifty
- ☐ Don't be wasteful of water, electricity, or other resources
- ☐ Reduce, Reuse, Recycle
- ☐ Use a less polluting product or method in your home, yard, school, business, or community
- ☐ Use mass transit/cycle/walk

SUPPORT OREGON'S ECONOMY
- ☐ Vacation in Oregon at least once a year
- ☐ Travel to a new part of Oregon
- ☐ Buy locally
- ☐ Buy Oregon products
- ☐ Educate yourself
- ☐ Figure out what watershed you live in
- ☐ Learn something about Oregon's history
- ☐ Learn CPR or first aid procedures
- ☐ Visit your local library

FOLLOW THE LAW, ALWAYS
- ☐ Don't jaywalk
- ☐ Give pedestrians the right-of-way
- ☐ Dispose of cigarette and cigar butts and ashtray contents properly
- ☐ Take the keys of someone who's intoxicated
- ☐ Completely stop for red and yellow lights and stop signs

GIVE OF YOURSELF AND YOUR RESOURCES

- ☐ Contribute to a school
- ☐ Engage a youth in a positive activity
- ☐ Adopt a senior or disabled citizen's home to keep up
- ☐ Help a senior citizen participate in a community activity
- ☐ Contact a local agency about assisting the homeless
- ☐ Create a community garden or neighborhood green space
- ☐ Contribute to charitable causes
- ☐ Give blood
- ☐ Deliver Meals on Wheels
- ☐ Serve on a non-profit board
- ☐ Be a mentor or Big Brother/Big Sister

SUPPORT OREGON'S EDUCATIONAL INSTITUTIONS AND CULTURAL ASSETS

- ☐ Recognize the work of a school or teacher
- ☐ Attend a cultural activity
- ☐ Visit a museum, historic site, or other cultural institution
- ☐ Leave artifacts untouched

PROMOTE SAFETY

- ☐ Make sure your guns are kept safely
- ☐ Support a law enforcement officer
- ☐ Know boating regulations and practice safe boating
- ☐ Follow hunter safety guidelines
- ☐ Stay off logs on the beach
- ☐ Learn to swim, and swim only in safe conditions

MAINTAIN AND IMPROVE OREGON'S HEALTH AND BEAUTY

- ☐ Don't litter or dump garbage
- ☐ Photograph, report, and then paint out graffiti
- ☐ Join a cleanup of Oregon's beaches, parks, roads, or natural areas
- ☐ Don't dump or hose waste down storm drains
- ☐ Leave a natural site better than you found it
- ☐ Plant a tree
- ☐ Don't walk by debris—pick it up
- ☐ Do something to encourage wildlife
- ☐ Don't target practice on signs or trees
- ☐ Stay on roads and trails
- ☐ Leave wildflowers and plants for others to enjoy
- ☐ Support conservation of open/green spaces

RESPECT YOUR FELLOW OREGONIANS

- ☐ Get to know someone different from yourself
- ☐ Practice kindness, manners, and patience
- ☐ Say thank you to service providers
- ☐ Give others the right-of-way when driving
- ☐ Smile often

MALHEUR COUNTY
One of the places to find thundereggs in Oregon.

OREGON ICONS
—

Oregonians have selected from the bounty of
natural resources "official" icons to represent the state.
Here's what's special about them.

STATE ROCK: Thundereggs

Nondescript on the outside, thundereggs reveal exquisite designs
in a wide range of colors when cut and polished. Thundereggs
range in diameter from less than one inch to more than four feet.
They are found chiefly in Crook, Jefferson, Malheur, Wasco, and
Wheeler Counties.

According to ancient Native American legend, when the
Thunder Spirits living in the highest recesses of snowcapped Mount
Hood and Mount Jefferson became angry with one another, amid
violent thunder and lightning storms they would hurl masses of
these spherical rocks at each other. The hostile gods obtained these
weapons by stealing eggs from the Thunderbirds' nests, thus the
source of the name "thundereggs."

Source: www.naturenw.org

STATE GEMSTONE: Oregon Sunstone

Oregon sunstones, a rare gem variety of the feldspar mineral
group, occur in Lake and Harney Counties where they are dug
from the soil and the underlying lava flows. Created in the
"shifting sand" of the Rabbit Hills located in the high desert
of Southeastern Oregon, the mineral content of the Oregon
sunstone differs from feldspar found any place else in the world.
Oregon sunstones are uncommon in their composition, clarity,
and range of colors.

Sunstone crystals as large as three inches across have been
found. In color, the gems range from water-clear through slight
yellow, blood red, orange-red, orange-pink, pink, and multi-color
which includes those with blue-green appearance. The sunstone
color relates to the amount of copper in the stone.

Source: www.cypac.com

STATE ANIMAL: American Beaver *(Castor canadensis)*

The American beaver was named Oregon state animal by the 1969 Legislature. Prized for its fur, the beaver was overtrapped by early settlers and eliminated from much of its original range. Through proper management and partial protection, the beaver has been reestablished in watercourses throughout the state and

remains an important economic asset. The beaver has been referred to as "nature's engineer," and its dam-building activities are important to natural water flow and erosion control. Oregon is known as the "Beaver State" and Oregon State University's athletic teams are called the "Beavers."

Source: *Oregon Blue Book*

"The beaver was the primary incentive for early exploration and it dominated the fur trade era in this part of the Northwest which finally led to settlement by a new class of immigrants. Its appropriateness is intensified also by its commonly accepted attributes. It is the universal symbol of thrift and industry and constructive endeavor—qualities as essential now as ever they were to the success of a people and a state."

MAY 25, 1925, *The Oregonian*
Source: www.users.fast.net

STATE BIRD: Western Meadowlark *(Sturnella neglecta)*

The western meadowlark was chosen state bird in 1927 by Oregon's school children in a poll sponsored by the Oregon Audubon Society. Native throughout western North America, the bird has brown plumage with buff and black markings. Its underside is bright yellow with a black crescent on the breast; its outer tail feathers are mainly white and are easily visible when it flies. The western meadowlark is known for its distinctive and beautiful song. Source: *Oregon Blue Book*

STATE FISH: Chinook Salmon *(Oncorhynchus tshawytscha)*

The Chinook salmon, also known as spring, king and tyee salmon, is the largest of the Pacific salmons and the most highly prized for the fresh fish trade. Declared state fish by the 1961 Legislature, the Chinook salmon is found from southern California to the Canadian Arctic. Record catches of 53 inches and 126 pounds have been reported. Source: *Oregon Blue Book*

> *"The common Salmon and red Charr [sockeye salmon] are the inhabitants of both the sea and rivers. The former is usually largest and weighs from 5 to 15 lbs. It is this species that extends itself into all the rivers and little creeks on this side of the Continent, and to which the natives are so much indebted for their subsistence."*

– MERIWETHER LEWIS, MARCH 13, 1806

STATE FLOWER: Oregon Grape
(Mahonia aquifolium)

A low growing plant, the Oregon grape is native to much of the Pacific Coast and is found sparsely east of the Cascades. Its year-round foliage of pinnated, waxy green leaves resembles holly, with fruit that looks like blueberries. The berries are edible and make an excellent wild jelly, providing you use *lots* of sugar! The inside of the stems and roots are colored bright yellow.

Early settlers knew Oregon grape well. They ate the fresh berries and, on south Vancouver Island, used them as an antidote to shellfish poisoning. Some boiled the outer bark of the roots to make a bright yellow dye for baskets. Liquid from the bark of boiled woody stems also helped treat red, itchy eyes.

Oregon's Governor's Mansion in Salem, Mahonia Hall, is named for the state flower.

Source: http://rbcm1.rbcm.gov.bc.ca (Royal British Columbia Museum)

STATE INSECT: Oregon Swallowtail *(Papilio oregonius)*

A true native of the Northwest, the Oregon swallowtail is at home in the lower sagebrush canyons of the Columbia River and its tributaries, including the Snake River drainage. This strikingly beautiful butterfly, predominantly yellow, is a wary, strong flier, not easily captured.

A recommended viewing spot is along the banks of the Columbia River at Vantage, Washington, "where I-90 crosses the river." According to entomologist Robert Michael Pyle, "Purists who want to see it *in* Oregon may leave I-80 at The Dalles and seek spots where the basalt bluffs run down to the Columbia Gorge, and Tarragon grows along the terraces."

Source: www.econ.state.or.us

STATE MUSHROOM: Pacific Golden Chanterelle *(Cantharellus formosus)*

The Pacific golden chanterelle is a wild, edible fungi of high culinary value that is unique to the Pacific Northwest. More than 500,000 pounds of the Pacific golden chanterelles are harvested annually in Oregon, representing a large portion of the commercial mushroom business.

Edible mushrooms have been widely collected from the forests of the Pacific Northwest since European settlers began hunting for mushrooms they had collected in their homelands. (Some native tribes harvested a few mushroom species, but we lack evidence of their wide-spread consumption.) During the 1990s, commercial mushroom harvesting has expanded dramatically as international markets developed and forest workers sought means to supplement their income.

Source: www.fsl.orst.edu

STATE NUT: Hazelnut *(Corylus avellana)*

Oregon grows approximately 99 percent of the entire U.S. commercial crop of hazelnuts. The Oregon hazelnut, unlike wild varieties, grows on single-trunked trees up to 30 or 40 feet tall. Adding a unique texture and flavor to recipes and products, Oregon hazelnuts are preferred by chefs, bakers, confectioners, food manufacturers, and homemakers worldwide.

Oregon's Willamette Valley farmers have grown hazelnuts since 1858 when the nuts were called filberts, a term still used by many Oregonians. No matter what you call these mild, sweet gems, they are widely considered to be larger and tastier than those grown elsewhere around the world.

Source: www.westnut.com

STATE SEASHELL: Oregon Hairy Triton *(Fusitriton oregonensis)*

In 1848, a conchologist (shell expert) named Redfield named the Fusitriton oregonensis after the Oregon Territory. Commonly called the Oregon hairy triton, the shell is one of the largest found in the state, reaching lengths up to five inches. The shells are found from Alaska to California and wash up on the Oregon coast at high tide. The legislature named the state shell in 1991.

Source: *Oregon Blue Book*

STATE TREE: Douglas Fir
(Pseudotsuga menziesii)

The Douglas fir (Pseudotsuga menziesii), named for David Douglas, a 19th century Scottish botanist, was designated state tree in 1939. Great strength, stiffness, and moderate weight make it an invaluable timber product said to be stronger than concrete. Averaging up to 200' in height and six feet in diameter, heights of 325' and diameters of 15' can also be found.

Source: *Oregon Blue Book*

STATE BEVERAGE: Milk

Milk production and the manufacturing of dairy products contributes over $600 million to Oregon's economic well being each year. Four hundred dairy farm families, with the help of their 96,000 dairy cows, and the care of the 20 Oregon dairy processors throughout the state, consistently produce top quality dairy products for the consumers' enjoyment. Nearly 60 percent of the state's milk is sold as fluid, the remaining 40 percent goes into cheese, yogurt, sour cream, ice cream, butter, and other cultured products.

Source: www.dairyfarmersor.com

STATE DANCE: Square Dance

The square dance is an American institution. It began in New England when the first settlers and the immigrant groups that followed, brought with them their various national dances, which we now call folk dances, but which were the popular dances of the day in the countries of their origin—the schottische, the quadrille, the jigs and reels, and the minuet, to name a few. After a week of toil in building new homes and carving homes out of virgin forest, the settlers would gather in the community center on Saturday evening and enjoy dancing their old-world favorites.

The pioneer origins of the dance and the characteristic dress are deemed to reflect Oregon's heritage; the lively spirit of the dance exemplifies the friendly, free nature and enthusiasm that are a part of the Oregon character.

Sources: www.dosado.com, *Oregon Blue Book*

STATE MOTTO

"She Flies With Her Own Wings" was adopted by the 1987 Legislature as the state motto. The phrase originated with Judge Jessie Quinn Thornton and was pictured on the territorial seal in Latin: *Alis Volat Propiis*. The new motto replaces "The Union," which was adopted in 1957.

STATE SONG: "Oregon, My Oregon"

J.A. Buchanan of Astoria and Henry B. Murtagh of Portland wrote "Oregon, My Oregon," in 1920. With this song, Buchanan and Murtagh won a statewide competition sponsored by the Society of Oregon Composers, gaining statewide recognition. The song became the official state song in 1927.

STATE FLAG

Oregon has the distinction of being the only state in the union whose flag has a different pattern on the reverse side. Both sides have a field of navy blue with design in gold. The front picture includes a heart shaped shield with an eagle on top, surrounded by thirty-three stars, representing the number of states in 1859. The scene on the shield shows the sun setting over the Pacific Ocean, mountains, forests, and a covered wagon. A plow, wheat, and pick-ax represent farming and mining. Of the two ships shown, the one leaving is a British ship and the one arriving is a United States ship, representing trade. The eagle represents the United States. On a banner are the words "The Union," representing support for the United States. Finally, the flag is emblazoned with the words "State of Oregon" above the picture and the date of statehood, "1859," below. On the reverse side of the flag there appears a beaver, the state animal.

Source: www.50states.com

FELLOW OREGONIANS
BALD EAGLE, RUFOUS HUMMINGBIRD,
WESTERN PAINTED TURTLE, GREAT BLUE HERON,
OSPREY, AND PACIFIC CHORUS FROG

Illustrations by Barbara Macomber

OREGON HEROES

JOHN McLOUGHLIN, TABITHA MOFFAT BROWN, OSWALD WEST,
TOM McCALL, BARBARA ROBERTS, BILL BOWERMAN,
FRED MEYER, MARK HATFIELD, AND STEVE PREFONTAINE

OREGON HEROES
—

A few of the people who helped make Oregon great

JOHN McLOUGHLIN (1784-1857) *"The Father of Oregon"*

Dr. John McLoughlin came to the Pacific Northwest in 1824 as a representative of the Hudson's Bay Company, which was to furs what Nike is to running shoes. McLoughlin made great contributions to the early development of the Oregon Country. He came to the great Northwest to promote the Hudson's Bay Company but he became "The Father of Oregon." He struggled tirelessly to provide employment and food to the many needy emigrants who began flooding into the new Oregon Country. Hudson's Bay officials criticized him for his hard-headedness, to which McLoughlin replied, "But what else could I do as a man having a spark of humanity in my nature?" He was named the Father of Oregon by the 1957 Legislature.

Source: http://archweb.sos.state.or

TABITHA MOFFAT BROWN (1780-1858) *"The Mother of Oregon"*

Honored by the 1987 Legislature as the Mother of Oregon, Tabitha Moffat Brown "represents the distinctive pioneer heritage and the charitable and compassionate nature of Oregon's people." At 66 years of age, she financed her own wagon for the trip from Missouri to Oregon. The boarding school for orphans that she established later became known as Tualatin Academy and eventually was chartered as Pacific University.

Source: www.bluebook.state.or.us/facts

OSWALD WEST (1873-1960) *"Protector of Oregon's Natural Beauty"*

Governor Oswald West in 1913, recognizing the aesthetic and economic value of Oregon's coastline, succeeded in getting legislators to declare that all of the wet-sand areas of Oregon beaches should be reserved for public use. Theodore Roosevelt considered Oswald West to be "a man more intelligently alive to the beauty of nature than almost any other man I have ever met holding a high political office." In addition, while West was governor (1910-1914) the office of State Forester and the Bureau of Forestry were established, and the Fish Commission and Game Commission were created. Source: www.open.org/~/wvor/parks

TOM McCALL (1913-1983) *"Visionary for the future"*

Tom McCall was Oregon's 30th governor from 1967-1975. With his campaigns based on livability, noteworthy accomplishments of his administration included cleaning up the Willamette River; tougher land-use laws; a bill which ended the threat of private development on Oregon's beaches; the nation's first mandatory bottle-deposit law; and creative energy conservation measures. While addressing the Oregon Legislature, McCall said, "Oregon is an inspiration. Whether you come to it, or are born to it, you become entranced by our state's beauty, the opportunity she affords, and the independent spirit of her citizens."

McCall, along with other community leaders, established SOLV in 1969. Source: www.sos.state.or.us/governors/McCall/mccallbiography

BARBARA ROBERTS (b. 1936) *"Inspirational public service"*

Barbara Roberts was inaugurated as Oregon's first woman governor on January 14, 1991. She completed her term as thirty-fourth governor in 1995. A descendant of Oregon Trail pioneers, Barbara Roberts began her career of public service as an advocate for disabled children as she fought for the educational rights of her autistic son. She served for a decade as an elected school board member, and eventually became a member of the Oregon House of Representatives. Then she moved on to Secretary of State, and Governor of Oregon. Under her leadership, Oregon earned a national reputation for solid government management and for workforce and education innovations.

Source: www.sos.state.or.us/governors/Roberts/robertsbio

BILL BOWERMAN (1911-1999) *"An innovative Oregon idea"*

Mr. Bowerman's storied career spanned the length and breadth of not only Oregon athletics, but the world. As a coach, educator, inventor, and sports icon, Mr. Bowerman set a standard and work ethic unmatched in most sports. By now the story is lore: With some latex, leather, glue, and his wife's waffle iron, Mr. Bowerman developed the first lightweight outsole that would revolutionize the running shoe. His durable, stable, and light Waffle sole set a new standard for shoe performance. Mr. Bowerman and Phil Knight began showing up anywhere there was running going on, with Knight selling shoes from the trunk of his car. From these beginnings Nike was formed. Source: www.nikebiz.com

FRED MEYER (1886-1978) *"Business savvy and philanthropic legacy"*

Fred G. Meyer was born in 1886 into a family of Brooklyn grocers. He came to Portland in 1909 and started a door-to-door coffee retail outlet in a downtown street market, and later built the chain of retail stores bearing his name throughout the Pacific Northwest. When Mr. Meyer died in 1978 at the age of 92, his will established the Fred Meyer Charitable Trust. Now called the Meyer Memorial Trust, it is a private, independent foundation representing Mr. Meyer's personal philanthropy and has granted nearly $300,000,000 to Oregon institutions.

Source: www.mmt.org/fredmeyer.html

MARK HATFIELD (b. 1922) *"Bi-Partisan and ethical leadership"*

Mark Hatfield has been a student, teacher, and practitioner of the American political system for virtually his entire life. After two terms in the Oregon House of Representatives and two years in the Oregon Senate, he became the youngest Secretary of State in Oregon history in 1956 at age 34. He was elected governor of Oregon in 1958 and became the state's first two-term governor in the twentieth century when he was re-elected in 1962. In 1968, then-Governor Mark Hatfield was elected to the United States Senate as an outspoken critic of the war in Vietnam. He consistently opposed increases in military spending and United States military involvement abroad while focusing on improving health, education, and social services programs.

Source: www.speaking.com/speakers/markhatfield.html

Photo Credit: U.S. Senate Historical Office

STEVE PREFONTAINE (1951-1975) *"An inspirational native son"*

During his brief 24-year life span, Steve Prefontaine grew from hometown hero to record-setting college phenomenon to internationally acclaimed track star. In a similar span of years since his death in 1975, Pre has become the stuff of enduring legend. At no place is the celebration of Steve Prefontaine and his story more personal than in Coos Bay, Oregon, where he was born in 1951 and discovered his gift for running fast and far as a student at Marshfield High School. He owned every (8) American record between 2,000 and 10,000 meters and between two miles and six miles.

Source: www.prefontainerun.com

BUENA VISTA OUTLOOK
The Malheur National Wildlife Refuge, Harney County

OREGON TIMELINE

YEAR EVENT

13,000,000 B.C. A great upheaval of the earth's crust forms the Cascade Mountains.

13,000 -10,000 YEARS AGO The earliest known Native Americans inhabit such areas as Fort Rock and The Dalles, Mack Canyon on the Rogue River, and Yaquina Head on the Pacific Coast.

1500 Spanish sailors returning to Mexico from the Philippines are the first white people to see the Oregon Coast.

1543 Bartolome' Ferrelo (Spanish) is the first known explorer to visit the Oregon Coast.

1579 Sir Francis Drake likely sailed into Nehalem Bay in Tillamook County, looking for a route between the Pacific and Atlantic Oceans.

1603 Martin d'Aguilar sails along the Oregon Coast and sights a river where the Columbia is later discovered.

1707 A Spanish galleon sailing from Manila wrecks on the Oregon Coast at the base of Neahkahnie Mountain; beeswax from its cargo will be found for years to come.

1765 British Major Robert Rogers sends a petition to King George III, asking permission to explore the Northwest, a territory called "Ouragon."

1775 Spaniards Bruno de Heceta and Juan de la Bodega y Quadra land near present-day Grenville and claim the territory for Spain. They are the first recorded Europeans to stand on Northwest soil.

1778 Capt. James Cook makes landfall at Cape Foulweather and discovers the fur wealth of the Northwest Coast.

1788 Captain Robert Gray, first American landing in Oregon, arrives in Tillamook in the *Lady Washington*. Markus Lopius, first African American to set foot on Oregon soil, is aboard.

1790 Spain and Britain sign an agreement resolving the dispute over claims along the Northwest Coast in favor of the British.

1792   Robert Gray, on his second voyage to Oregon, enters the Columbia River, names it after his ship, the *Columbia Rediviva*.

1794   England and Spain amend their 1790 agreement, as Spain withdraws its claims to the Northwest.

PRE-1800S   Estimated annual runs of salmon and steelhead are 10-16 million fish.

1804-1806   Captains Meriwether Lewis and William Clark travel with their party from Missouri to the mouth of the Columbia River.

1811   John Jacob Astor founds Astoria as a fur trading post. It is the first white settlement in Oregon.

1818   The U.S. and England agree on "joint occupancy" of the Oregon Country.

1819   Treaty between U.S. and Spain fixes the Southern Oregon border at the 42nd parallel.

1821   The Hudson's Bay Company acquires a fur monopoly for all of British North America after merging with the North West Company. It remains the most influential non-native power in the Northwest for the next 25 years.

1825   David Douglas begins botanical collecting.

1827   Dr. John McLoughlin, Hudson's Bay Company agent, builds the Northwest's first sawmill. U.S. and Great Britain agree to indefinite "joint occupancy."

1829   Dr. John McLoughlin establishes claim at Willamette Falls, later Oregon City.

1833   First lumber exports by Hudson's Bay Company to China.

1837   The Willamette Cattle Company is formed, marking the first cooperative venture among Oregon settlers.

1839   First printing press is brought to the Northwest from Honolulu and used to print a Nez Perce primer.

1840   Population of Americans in Oregon Territory = 150 (estimated).

1842   Willamette University is founded, making it the first university west of the Mississippi.

1843   Settlers of the Oregon Territory form provisional government. Joseph Meek swings the vote at the Champoeg meeting on May 2.

1843   The first large group of Americans arrives over the Oregon Trail.

1843   Clackamas, Marion, Yamhill, and Tuality (renamed to Washington in 1849) Counties established.

1844 Clatsop County established.
1844 Oregon City is selected as the first capital of Oregon Country.
1845 Polk County established.
1846 Treaty defines the 49th parallel as the boundary between British and U.S. Territory.
1847 Linn and Benton Counties are established.
1848 Oregon Territory is created as a political unit of the U.S.
1850 Congress passes the Oregon Donation Law, restricting land claims to 320 acres for a white male and 320 acres for his wife.
1850 Oregon population = 12,093.
1851 Lane County established.
1851-1852 Gold is found along Jackson Creek in southern Oregon.
1852 Douglas and Jackson Counties established.
1853 A treaty creates the first Indian reservation in the territory.
1853 Coos and Tillamook Counties established.
1854 Columbia, Wasco, and Multnomah Counties established.
1855 Curry County established.
1856 Josephine County established.
1857 Climbers reach the summit of Mount Hood for the first time.
1859 Congress admits Oregon as the 33rd state on February 14.
1859 Steamboat passenger service is extended along the Columbia River as far as The Dalles.
1860 Oregon population = 52,465.
1860 Daily stagecoach service begins between Portland and Sacramento.
1862 Umatilla and Baker Counties established.
1864 Union and Grant Counties established.
1864 A salmon-canning factory is built in Astoria.
1865 The Silverton fire burns one million acres, the largest known in Oregon's history.
1866 A paper mill begins operating in Oregon City.
1868 Corvallis College (now Oregon State University) becomes the first state-supported institution of higher education in Oregon.
1869 Direct export of wheat to Europe begins.
1869 Oregon's first public high school is established in Portland.
1870 There are 173 sawmills in Oregon, 138 of which use water power.
1870 Oregon population = 90,923.
1871 Abigail Scott Duniway introduces Susan B. Anthony in Oregon to galvanize a women's suffrage crusade.

1874 Lake County created from Jackson and Wasco Counties.
1876 University of Oregon opens in Eugene.
1878 Women gain right to vote in school elections.
1880 Oregon population = 174,768.
1882 Klamath and Crook Counties established.
1885 Women gain admittance to law practice.
1885 Gilliam and Morrow Counties established.
1885 A transplanted New Englander plants the first cranberry bog on the Pacific Coast in Coos County.
1887 Malheur and Wallowa Counties established.
1887 The first Pacific Northwest salmon hatchery is established in Oregon.
1889 Sherman and Harney Counties established.
1890 Oregon population = 317,704.
1892 The Portland Art Association is founded.
1893 Lincoln County established.
1896 The Portland Symphony Orchestra is born.
1899 Wheeler County established.
1900 Oregon population = 413,536.
1902 Crater Lake National Park is created.
1902 More than 110 forest fires from Eugene, Oregon to Bellingham, Washington burn an estimated 700,000 acres.
1903 Oregonians enact a law giving women workers a 10-hour day.
1905 The Portland Art Museum opens.
1908 Hood River County created from Wasco County.
1909 Oregon Caves National Monument established.
1910 Oregon population = 672,765.
1910 Jantzen Knitting Mills created.
1912 Women's suffrage is adopted in Oregon.
1913 Governor Oswald West declares beaches open to the public.
1914 Eight-hour day approved for women.
1914 Jefferson County created from a portion of Crook County.
1916 Deschutes County created from a portion of Crook County.
1920 Oregon population = 783,389.
1930 Oregon population = 953,786.
1933 Tillamook Burn destroys 300,000 acres of timber.
1936 First woman, Nan Wood Honeyman, elected from Oregon to House of Representatives.
1937 Oregon Shakespeare Festival forms in Ashland.
1940 Oregon population = 1,089,684.

1942 Women are called to jury duty in a federal court for the first time in Oregon.

1948 A flood on Memorial Day obliterates the town of Vanport, a Portland suburb of 17,500 built to house wartime workers.

1948 Howard Vollum and Jack Murdock found Tektronix, Inc.

1949 Portland elects its first woman mayor, Dorothy McCullough Lee.

1950 Oregon population = 1,521,341.

1955 Portland State College established.

1960 Oregon population = 1,768,687.

1960 First woman Oregon senator, Maurine Neuberger, elected.

1962 The "Columbus Day Storm" causes extensive damage as wind gusts reach 96 miles per hour.

1965 Portland State College upgraded to University.

1967 Oregon Beach Bill signed into law making Oregon unique among coastal states by guaranteeing public access to the entire coastline.

1968 The Nike company is established.

1969 Department of Environmental Quality created.

1970 Oregon population = 2,091,533.

1971 The nation's first mandatory Bottle Bill is passed by the Oregon legislature.

1974 John Day Fossil Beds National Monument is established.

1975 Congress creates Hells Canyon National Recreation Area.

1980 Mount St. Helens erupts in southwestern Washington.

1980 Oregon population = 2,633,321.

1982 First woman, Betty Roberts, appointed justice of Oregon Supreme Court.

1985 First woman, Vera Katz, selected speaker of Oregon House.

1986 Metropolitan Area Express (MAX) begins light-rail service in Portland.

1990 Oregon population = 2,842,321.

1991 Barbara Roberts is inaugurated as Oregon's first woman Governor.

1992 First African-American, James A. Hill, Jr., elected to state office.

1993 First statewide vote-by-mail election held in U.S.

1996 Oregon conducts the first vote-by-mail election for a federal office.

2000 Oregon population = 3,421,399.

2025 Oregon population = 4,349,000 (projected).

Sources: www.webtrail.com/applegate/oregonbluebook.state.or.us/cultural/history/chronhome
www.endoftheoregontrail.org/blaktimeeducation.opb.org/learning/oregonstory/logging/timeline

PONDEROSA PINE
Deschutes National Forest, Deschutes County

WHEN I'M AWAY FROM OREGON FOR A FEW DAYS, WHAT I MISS THE MOST IS...

"the mountains, and having a sure sense of place."
— ANNE MADDEN, CEDAR MILL

"the respect people show for one another and their surroundings."
— LAURIE SHAW, TIGARD

"all the beautiful trees and nature surrounding us."
— CLAIRE DUNN, PORTLAND

"all my friends and family."
— KATIE DUNN, BEAVERTON

"the wide, open spaces and the people that are working to preserve them."
— BOONE JOHNSON, PORTLAND

"crisp air flavored with mist, sweet, cool, drinkable water, and a view of white cap Mt. Hood."
— CLEO RUMPAKIS, PORTLAND

———

"There is an aroma to the beaches of Oregon that is not to be matched anywhere in the world. It is a fresh, clean aroma touched with the essence of salt spray, seaweed, sand, and that mysterious ingredient I can't identify."

— THOMAS W. CUTSFORTH, FOSSIL

AN OREGON BOUNTY
Yamhill County

A FEW SPECIAL FACTS AND CURIOSITIES ABOUT OREGON

OREGON'S VINEYARDS AND WINERIES

The largest concentration of Oregon's 193 wineries is located in the Willamette Valley wine region, which stretches from Portland to Eugene, between the Cascade Mountains and the Coastal Range. The Umpqua Valley, Applegate Valley, and Rogue Valley wine regions are located in the southwestern portion of the state. Small portions of the Columbia Valley and Walla Walla Valley wine regions lie in Oregon. Both of these two regions, however, lie mostly within Washington State.

More than 10,500 acres of vines exist in Oregon today, up from 35 acres in 1970. Oregon ranks second in the United States for number of wineries, and fourth in production.

The Oregon wine grape crop totaled a record high 18,600 tons, up four percent from 1999 and 27 percent higher than 1998. Wine sales in Oregon in the year 2000 were $120 million, or 991,770 cases.

A NATIVE OREGONIAN

Ariolimax columbianus, commonly known as the banana slug, is so named for its coloring resembling a banana. Bright yellow body with black spots, it is the second largest slug in the world, growing up to 10 inches in length.

Well-known for their slime (accidentally stepping on a slug in one's bare feet has produced legendary tales from Oregonians), the banana slug relies on its coating for movement, defense, water retention, and reproduction.

Source: http:bss.sfsu.edu

BEERVANA

Oregon is home to more than 70 microbreweries, with Portland taking credit for more than one-third that number. In fact, Portland has more microbreweries and brewpubs per capita than any other city in the United States. With so many options, you're never more than 10-15 minutes from a pint of locally brewed beer.

Oregon's mild climate, similar to that of Europe's growing regions, is ideal for producing top-of-the-line ingredients. Oregon produces 17 percent of the nation's hops and 4 percent of the world's hops. Recognizing these benefits granted by Mother Nature, breweries throughout the United States and the world look to Oregon for hops that will satisfy the tastes of today's sophisticated beer drinker.

Source: www.pova.com (Portland Oregon Visitor's Association)

BERRY GOOD

If you're an Oregon cranberry, chances are good that your family roots can be traced to the southern Oregon coast. Oregon is the fourth major producer of cranberries in the United States, with most Oregon cranberries growing in the Bandon and Port Orford area. A smaller percentage is also grown north of Tillamook along the coast.

Oregon cranberries are known for their bright red color obtained from the mild climate of the area, due to the influence of the Pacific Ocean. This allows the berries to stay on the vine much longer than other growing regions.

Cranberries have been grown in Oregon since 1885, when Charles McFarlin planted vines he brought from Massachusetts. He had originally come to pan for gold in California. He didn't make his fortune, or even a living, so he turned to what he knew best. He brought vines from Cape Cod and planted them in the state's first cranberry bog near Hauser, in Coos County.

Sources: http://members.aol.com

O, CHRISTMAS TREE!

Oregon is the nation's leader in Christmas tree production. The industry has a value of $135 million and is one of the state's top commodities. Oregon's 600+ growers are concentrated in the Willamette Valley, but there are licensed growers in many other counties, including some east of the Cascades.

Douglas fir is still the mainstay of Oregon production, although the noble fir remains popular as well. Oregon soils and climate are conducive to growing a quality Christmas tree, with an average of 2,000 trees planted per acre. At six to seven feet, trees are ready for harvest. It takes six to ten years of fighting heavy rain, wind, hail, and drought to get a mature tree.

Over 8 million Christmas trees are currently harvested in the state each year. Buyers include retail chains, street corner lots, and resellers; however, Oregon's population is not large enough to consume more than a few hundred-thousand trees. That's why so many need to leave the state. Oregon Christmas trees arrive yearly in Asia, the South Pacific, Canada, and Mexico.

Sources: http://ms.essortment.com, http://ww.oda.state.or.us
http://www.urbantext.uiuc.edu/trees/treefacts

OREGON'S FAMOUS RAIN

BY VALERIE LANTZ, TROUTDALE

EXPERIENCE OREGON rain. It comes in many forms. Downpour, sprinkle, steady drizzle, mist, or a few drops in the dust. Walk along a foggy riverfront path in Astoria. Drive past miles of dry sagebrush near Fields. Take a bike ride in light rain along the Bear Creek Greenway near Medford. Saddle a horse for a ride past Eagle Cap Mountain and dodge a thunderstorm. Each place possesses its own character and a different kind of rain. Oregon's unique rainfall patterns and the land that it falls upon provide special landscape diversity worth preserving.

The Columbia River Gorge demonstrates how rain turns barren rock into lush garden. As the rainfall decreases from west to east, the rock formations become more and more stark. Preserving the Gorge as a National Scenic Area provides opportunities for experiencing forest-covered cliffs with every waterfall shape represented. Generous rainfall feeds the waterfalls on the Gorge's western end. Traveling east finds drier, open country filled with wildflowers. People travel from countries around the world to see the Columbia River Gorge. Visitors experience landscape changes from Troutdale to Hood River and then more changes when approaching The Dalles. Rain and sun combine for spectacular rainbows from the Rowena overlook.

Other locations all around the state represent unique natural areas, each with different kinds of landforms combined with wide variations in rainfall. The rich diversity of landscapes within Oregon makes this state special. The diverse landscapes are worth preserving.

OREGON EVENTS

IF YOU want to be inspired by Oregon and Oregonians, try visiting a special community event. You'll meet the people who live there and experience first-hand some of what makes the place special. For contact information, visit www.oregon.com.

JANUARY

Winter Whale Watch – *entire coast*
Annual Artistry in Wood Show – *Lincoln City*
Crab & Chowder Festival – *Turner*
Scottish New Years Feast – *Cave Junction*
Horse-drawn elk viewing excursions – *North Powder*

FEBRUARY

Chocolate & Coffee Lovers Festival – *Seaside*
Oregon Shakespeare Festival – *Ashland (February to October)*
Oregon Wine & Food Festival – *Salem*
Seafood & Wine Festival – *Newport*

MARCH

Daffodil Festival – *Junction City*
Dixieland Clambake Jazz Festival – *North Bend*
Spring Fair – *Roseburg*
Tulip Festival – *Woodburn (March/April)*

APRIL

Crab & Seafood Festival – *Warrenton*
Family Science Festival – *Bend*
Migratory Bird Festival – *Burns*
Oregon Ag Fest – *Salem*
Pear Blossom Festival – *Medford*
Puffin Kite Festival – *Cannon Beach*
Scottish Heritage Festival – *Salem*
Sea Lion Suds Fest – *Gold Beach*

MAY

Azalea Festival – *Brookings*
Clam Chowder Festival – *Gold Beach*
Iris Festival Days & Parade – *Keizer*
Memorial Day Festival – *Wasco*
Molalla Festival of Art – *Molalla*
Rhododendron Festival – *Florence*
Strawberry Festival – *Lebanon (May/June)*
Sumpter Valley Country Fair – *Sumpter*
Whale of a Wine Festival – *Gold Beach*
Wildflower Festival – *Coos Bay*

JUNE

Basque Festival – *Burns*
Beachcomber Days Festival – *Waldport*
Big River Band Festival – *Arlington*
Cascade Music Festival – *Lincoln City*
Crab Festival – *Wheeler*
Dairy Festival & Rodeo – *Tillamook*
Dragon Boat Races – *Portland*
Festival of Balloons – *Tigard*
Festival of Bands – *Portland*
Festival of Free Flight – *Lakeview (June/July)*
Festival of Gardens – *Lincoln City*
Frazier Farmstead Wine & Food Tasting Festival –
   Milton-Freewater
Grand Floral Parade – *Portland*
Junior Rose Festival Parade – *Portland*
Oregon Bach Festival – *Eugene (June/July)*
Portland Arts Festival – *Portland*
Rose Festival Air Show – *Hillsboro*
Rose Festival CART Races – *Portland*
Scandinavian Midsummer Festival – *Astoria*
Showcase of Floats – *Portland*
Starlight Parade – *Portland*
Strawberry Festival – *Wilsonville*
Summer Festival – *Roseburg*

OFFICE OF THE GOVERNOR

From the first Oregonians who crossed the Bering Land Bridge thousands of years ago, to those who struggled along the Oregon Trail, to those who come today on blacktop freeways, the promise of this good land still calls. We, who call Oregon home, are all seeking a better life for ourselves, and for our children.

This remarkable land gives us all so much and asks for so little in return. One way to show our collective gratitude for our home is to find ways of contributing to the continuing health and livability of Oregon. Each of us can take part in SOLV activities: there are projects being organized in your local community. Read to a child or join local food drives for those who are less fortunate. Contribute time and resources to non-profit organizations. In short, become more involved in your Oregon.

It doesn't matter if you're Republican, Democrat, Libertarian or Independent. It doesn't matter if your community is urban or rural. The one thing which binds all of us is that Oregon is our home and we must work together to make it better. Let this shared desire become a rallying call for a new, renewed spirit that will make a better Oregon for today and for future generations.

Each one of us can be a participant in this building process. In this manual, you will find 12 practices which hundreds of your fellow citizens from across the State felt were important statements about living in Oregon. Please review them and see how you can be involved.

If we work together, if we can develop a new, shared vision; we can send a worldwide statement about the New Oregon, where we have once again reclaimed the spirit which defines this good land as no other.

Welcome to the journey!

Theodore R. Kulongoski
Governor of Oregon

JULY

Annual Basset Hound Olympics – *Lebanon*
Bohemia Mining Days – *Cottage Grove*
Central Oregon Draft Horse Show – *Redmond*
Chief Joseph Days & Rodeo – *Joseph*
Country Faire & Carnival – *Bonanza*
da Vinci Days – *Corvallis*
Dallas Summerfest – *Dallas*
Elgin Stampede PRCA Rodeo – *Elgin*
Fireworks & Music Festival – *Waldport*
Golden Years Festival – *Coburg*
High Desert Marine Walleye Derby – *Boardman*
Japan Nite Obon Festival – *Ontario*
Leaburg Festival – *Leaburg*
Miners Jubilee Celebration – *Baker City*
Molalla Buckeroo Rodeo – *Molalla*
Mosquito Festival – *Paisley*
Newberg Old-Fashion Festival – *Newberg*
Obon & Taiko Drumming Festival – *Eugene*
Ocean Festival – *Winchester Bay*
Oregon Brewers Festival – *Portland*
Oregon Coast Music Festival – *Coos Bay*
Oregon Country Fair – *Veneta*
Pioneer Heritage Festival – *Baker City*
Portland Highland Scottish Games – *Portland*
Sisters Outdoor Quilt Show – *Sisters*
Southern Oregon Kite Festival – *Brookings*
State Games of Oregon – *Portland*
Summer Blues Festival – *Roseburg*
Summer Festival – *Toledo*
Summer in the City – *Salem*
Sumpter Valley Country Fair – *Sumpter*
Taste of Beaverton – *Beaverton*
The Robin Hood Festival – *Sherwood*
Waterfront Blues Festival – *Portland*
Watermelon Festival – *Irrigon*
Western Days Old-Fashioned Fourth –
   Independence/Monmouth
Wildhorse PowWow – *Pendleton*
Yachats Annual Smelt Fry – *Yachats*

AUGUST

Annual Charleston Seafood Festival – *Charleston*
Annual Salmon Barbecue – *Charleston*
Annual Sandcastle Building Contest – *Lincoln City*
Antique Fair & Folk Music Festival – *Toledo*
Astoria Regatta Festival – *Astoria*
Blackberry Arts Festival – *Coos Bay*
Blackberry Festival – *Sutherlin*
Blues Festival – *Brooks*
Charleston Seafood Festival – *Charleston*
Elephant Garlic Festival – *North Plains*
Huckleberry Festival & Trail Days – *Welches*
Jedediah Smith Rendezvous – *Grants Pass*
Late Summer Bluegrass Festival – *Odell*
Mexican Fiesta – *Woodburn*
Mt. Hood Jazz Festival – *Gresham*
Muddy Frogwater Country Classic Festival –
  Milton-Freewater
Nehalem Art Festival – *Nehalem*
Nesika Illahee Pow Wow – *Siletz*
North American Jew's Harp Festival – *Richland*
NW Art & Air Festival – *Albany*
Old Tyme Arts & Crafts Fair – *Waldport*
Open Air Antique Fair – *Oregon City*
Oregon Trail Days/Old Time Fiddle Contest – *LaGrande*
Restoration Celebration – *Chiloquin*
Santiam Canyon Stampede & Summerfest – *Stayton*
Scandinavian Festival – *Junction City*
Springfield Filbert Festival – *Springfield*
Tail End Pooch Parade – *Multnomah Village*, *Portland*
Vernonia Friendship Jamboree – *Vernonia*
Wild Blackberry Festival – *Cave Junction*
Wine & Blues Festival – *Veneta*

SEPTEMBER

Alpenfest – *Joseph*
Annual Indian Salmon Bake – *Depoe Bay*
Art & Seafood Festival – *Port Orford*
Asian Kite Festival – *Eugene*
Bay Area Fun Festival – *Coos Bay*

Coburg Antique Fair – *Coburg*
Crab Festival & Chowder Cook-Off – *Waldport*
Cranberry Festival – *Bandon*
Eugene Oktoberfest – *Eugene*
Festival of Quilts – *Gold Beach*
Harvest Faire – *Troutdale*
Harvest Festival – *Myrtle Point*
Lewis & Clark Kite Exposition – *Seaside*
Melon Festival – *Winston*
Mt. Angel Oktoberfest – *Mt. Angel*
Oregon Coast Air Fair – *North Bend*
Pendleton Round-Up – *Pendleton*
Polish Festival – *Portland*
Salmon Festival – *Wheeler*
Sand Sculpture & Beach Festival – *Seaside*
Shrewsbury Renaissance Faire – *Albany*
Shorebird Festival – *Coos Bay*
Sumpter Valley Country Fair – *Sumpter*
Walterville Community Fair – *Walterville*
Wine, Art, & Music Festival – *Roseburg*

OCTOBER
Annual Sisters Harvest Faire – *Sisters*
Apple Festival – *Molalla*
Applegate Trail Wagon Train Re-enactment Celebration –
    Sunny Valley
Brocards Antique Cider Press – *Sweet Home*
Great Oregon Beach Cleanup – *entire coast*
Hood River Valley Harvest Festival– *Hood River*
Hot Air Balloon Bash – *Pendleton*
Lincoln City Glass Float Distribution + Glass Float
    Odyssey – *Lincoln City*
Onion Festival – *Sherwood*
Salmon Festival – *Troutdale*
Scarecrow Festival – *Milton-Freewater*
Scarecrow Village Harvest Festival – *Salem*
Yachats Village Mushroom Fest – *Yachats*

NOVEMBER

Audubon Wild Arts Festival – *Portland*
Christmas Caroling & Lighted Float Parade – *Seaside*
Christmas Fair – *Roseburg (November/December)*
Christmas on the Prairie Festival – *Prairie City*
Doll & Toy Festival – *Eugene*
Festival of Trees – *Eugene*
Festival of Trees – *Portland (November/December)*
Grape & Grain Festival with Art Auction – *John Day*
Holiday Food & Gift Festival – *Eugene*
Holiday Food & Gift Festival – *Portland*
Holiday Food & Gift Festival – *Redmond*
Mt. Hood Railroad Thanksgiving Special & Turkey Bowling
  Contest – *Mt. Hood*
Oregon Coast Aquarium's Sea of Lights Holiday Party –
  Newport
Philomath Frolic & Rodeo Craft Fair – *Philomath*
Polk County Craft Festival – *Rickreall*
Stormy Weather Arts Festival – *Cannon Beach*
Wine & Arts Festival – *Welches*
Wine Country Thanksgiving – *Yamhill County*
Winter Ale Festival – *Portland (November/December)*

DECEMBER

Community Tree Lighting – *Monmouth*
Festival of Lights – *Eugene*
Nature's Coastal Holiday Light Festival – *Brookings*
The Grotto's Festival of Lights – *Portland*
Victorian Christmas – *Jacksonville*
Victorian Holiday Festival – *Eugene*
Winter Whale Watch Week – *entire coast*
ZooLights – *Portland*

OREGON COUNTIES

—

Experience Oregon's beauty and diversity
through her 36 counties.

Data provided courtesy of the Oregon Blue Book
*Geographic pronunciations courtesy
of www.bartleby.com and Dale Archibald*

Baker

COUNTY SEAT: 1995 3rd St., Baker City 97814
PHONE: 541-523-8207
WEB: www.bakercounty.org
ESTABLISHED: Sep. 22, 1862
ELEV. AT BAKER CITY: 3,471'
AREA: 3,089 sq. mi.
AVERAGE TEMP.: Jan. 25.2°, July 66.6°
ANNUAL PRECIPITATION: 10.63"
ECONOMY: Agriculture, forest products, manufacturing, and recreation.

POINTS OF INTEREST: The Oregon Trail Interpretive Center and Old Oregon Trail, Sumpter Gold Dredge Park and ghost towns, Sumpter Valley Railroad, Baker City Restored Historic District, Anthony Lakes Ski Resort, Eagle Cap Wilderness Area, Brownlee, Oxbow and Hells Canyon Reservoirs and Hells Canyon (deepest gorge in the U.S.).

GEOGRAPHIC PRONUNCIATIONS	
Durkee	DUR-kee
Sumpter	SUMP-tur

"Baker City is a wonderful place to live and visit. Beautiful scenery, excellent schools, great merchants, unlimited recreational opportunities, and clean, healthy, safe living conditions are among the many blessings that we enjoy. Our most valuable asset is our citizens. They are friendly, helpful, and consistently demonstrating a positive 'can-do' approach to life."

— NANCY SHARK, MAYOR, BAKER CITY

Early winter storms bring fresh snow to the **ELKHORN MOUNTAINS** that guard **BAKER VALLEY.**

"September 6, 1862, a day to remember, we arrived at Flagstaff
Hill overlooking Powder Valley. Coming over this last hill a
most remarkable sight met our eyes. Here was a beautiful valley
with luxuriant growth of green grass through which flowed a
river of clear sparkling water with high mountains in the rear.
The grass was even better than that cultivated in the rich soil
of north Missouri. On the west side of the river was rye grass so
high you could ride through on a small horse and never be seen.
A land the likes of which I never seen and I decided, 'Here is
where I am going to live!'"

– A PIONEER FROM THE FIRST WAGON TRAIN TO ARRIVE IN BAKER CITY, 1862

Benton

COUNTY SEAT: 120 NW Fourth St., Corvallis 97330

PHONE: 541-766-6831

WEB: www.co.benton.or.us

ESTABLISHED: Dec. 23, 1847

ELEV. AT CORVALLIS: 224'

AREA: 679 sq. mi.

AVERAGE TEMP.: Jan. 39.3°, July 65.6°

ANNUAL PRECIPITATION: 42.71"

ECONOMY: Agriculture, forest products, research and development, electronics, and wineries.

POINTS OF INTEREST: Oregon State University, Alsea Falls, Mary's Peak, William L. Finley National Wildlife Refuge, Peavy Arboretum, McDonald Forest, Jackson Frazier Wetland.

GEOGRAPHIC PRONUNCIATIONS	
Philomath	fi-LO-muth
Corvallis	kor-VAL-is
Alsea	AL-see

"...it is springtime, 1847...The past winter there has been a strange fever raging here. It is the Oregon Fever. It seems to be contagious... Nothing seems to stop it, but to tear up and take a 6 month trip across the plains with ox team to the Pacific Ocean..."

– FROM DIARY OF KETURAH BELKNAP, EARLY SETTLER OF BENTON COUNTY, BENTON COUNTY HISTORICAL MUSEUM, PHILOMATH, OREGON
Source: www.peak.org/~lewisb/

"Only when I began studying chemical engineering at Oregon Agricultural College did I realize that I myself might discover something new about the nature of the world."

– LINUS PAULING, NOBEL PRIZE IN CHEMISTRY, 1954, OSU GRADUATE, BENTON COUNTY

COVERED BRIDGES

OREGON HAS the largest collection of covered bridges in the western part of the United States, with more than 50 extant covered spans. Because of the easy availability of forest resources in Oregon, most of the early bridges in the state were timber structures. These timber bridges were often covered to protect them from the weather. Now, the remaining examples of this obsolete bridge construction technology, generally located in pastoral rural settings, provide one of the most significant tourist attractions in the state.

The Harris Bridge would seem to exemplify the romantic notion of the covered bridge. This Howe truss span of seventy-five feet bridges the Marys River on a winding graveled country lane at an idyllic pastoral townsite named after George Harris, whose family settled the area in 1890. The current bridge was built in 1936 to replace the original covered bridge on the site.

Sources: www.odot.state.or.us, http://coveredbridges.stateoforegon.com

LARWOOD COVERED BRIDGE
Willamette Valley

SHIMANEK COVERED BRIDGE
Linn County

Clackamas

COUNTY SEAT: Board of Commissioners' Office, 906 Main St., Oregon City 97045

PHONE: 503-655-8698

WEB: www.co.clackamas.or.us

ESTABLISHED: July 5, 1843

ELEV. AT OREGON CITY: 55'

AREA: 1,879 sq. mi.

AVERAGE TEMP.: Jan. 40.2°, July 68.4°

ANNUAL PRECIPITATION: 48.40"

ECONOMY: Agriculture, metals manufacturing, trucking and warehousing, nursery stock, retail services, wholesale trade, and construction.

POINTS OF INTEREST: Mt. Hood and Timberline Lodge, End of the Oregon Trail Interpretive Center, Willamette Falls and Locks, McLoughlin House, Canby Ferry.

GEOGRAPHIC PRONUNCIATIONS	
Clackamas	KLAK-uh-mus
Estacada	es-tuh-KAY-duh
Lake Oswego	ahs-WEE-go
Molalla	mo-LA-la

Clackamas received its name from the Clackamas Indians, a Chinookan tribe, living along the river. One of the original four districts of early Oregon, along with Tuality, Yamhill, and Champooick.
Source: *Oregon Geographic Names*

Responding to an advertisement on June 12, 1894:

"To Mountain Climbers and Lovers of Nature...It has been decided to meet on the summit of Mt. Hood on the 19th of next month..."

More than 300 people encamped on the flanks of Mt. Hood on July 18. By 8:00 a.m. the next day, the first climbing party reached the 11,239' summit, followed by the rest of the 193 men and women who were to reach the summit that day.
Source: www.mazamas.org

JOHNSRUD VIEWPOINT is an Oregon Trail interpretive site;
View of the Sandy River Valley, and majestic Mt. Hood.

*"Here I am on the slopes of Mount Hood where
I have always wanted to come."*

FRANKLIN D. ROOSEVELT, SEPTEMBER 28, 1937,
DEDICATION OF TIMBERLINE LODGE

Clatsop

COUNTY SEAT: Courthouse, 749 Commercial St., Astoria 97103

PHONE: 503-325-8511

WEB: www.co.clatsop.or.us

ESTABLISHED: June 22, 1844

ELEV. AT ASTORIA: 19'

AREA: 843 sq. mi.

AVERAGE TEMP.: Jan. 41.9°, July 60.1°

ANNUAL PRECIPITATION: 66.40"

ECONOMY: Fishing, tourism, and forest products.

POINTS OF INTEREST: Astoria Column, Port of Astoria, Flavel Mansion Museum, Lewis and Clark Expedition Salt Cairn, Fort Clatsop, Fort Stevens, Columbia River Maritime Museum.

GEOGRAPHIC PRONUNCIATIONS	
Clatsop	KLAT-suhp
Necanicum	ne-KAN-i-com
Klaskanine	KLATS-ka-nye
Tolovanna	TOL-uh-van-ah

ASTORIA COLUMN

The Astoria Column, in a wooded park atop Astoria's highest hill, presents a spectacular view of the historic city and its surrounding rivers, bay, forest, mountains, and ocean. The Column, built in 1926, is 125 feet high and has 164 steps winding to the top. The Column presents a fascinating illustration of the discovery of the Columbia River by Captain Robert Gray in 1792, the establishment of American claims to the Northwest Territory, the winning of the West, and the arrival of the Great Northern Railway.

"Astoria, the oldest American town west of the Rockies, is an historic feast for the senses. Located on the Columbia River, where this mighty River of the West empties into the Pacific Ocean, Astoria is the site where Lewis and Clark wintered in 1805 at the end of their Journey of Discovery and where New York Financier John Jacob Astor established a trading post in 1811. It also has the distinction of having the first U.S. Post Office west of the Rockies, established in 1847. More than one-fourth of its houses are eligible for Historic Landmark status."

— JOHN COMPERE, ASTORIA

PORT OF ASTORIA
The last ray of a storm-threatened sunset cast a radiant light on ships and cranes.

"At 4 a.m., saw the entrance of our desired port bearing east-south-east, distance six leagues; in steering sails, and hauled our wind in shore. At 8 a.m., being a little to the windward of the entrance to the harbor, bore away, and run in east-north-east, between the breakers...When we were over the bar we found this to be a large river of fresh water up which we steered."

– LOG BOOK ENTRY OF THE SHIP COLUMBIA FOR MAY 11, 1792 (SAILED INTO THE COLUMBIA RIVER, CAPTAIN GRAY IN COMMAND). Source: *Oregon Historical Quarterly*, Vol. 1, No. 2, June 1900, Joseph R. Wilson

"Great joy in camp we are in View of the Ocian, this great Pacific Ocean which we been So long anxious to See."

– CAPTAIN WILLIAM CLARK, NOVEMBER 7, 1805

"Without wishing to deprive any other portion of Oregon, it may fairly be conceded that Astoria has before it the certainty of a wealthy and prosperous [future]." Source: *The Oregonian*, June 16, 1855

Columbia

COUNTY SEAT: Courthouse,
St. Helens 97051-0010
PHONE: 503-397-3796
WEB: www.co.columbia.or.us
ESTABLISHED: Jan. 16, 1854
ELEV. AT ST. HELENS: 42'
AREA: 687 sq. mi.
AVERAGE TEMP.: Jan. 39.0°, July 68.4°
ANNUAL PRECIPITATION: 44.60"
ECONOMY: Agriculture, forest products,
manufacturing, surface mining,
and tourism.

POINTS OF INTEREST: Lewis and
Clark Heritage Canoe Trail, Jewell Elk
Refuge, Sauvie Island Wildlife Area.

GEOGRAPHIC PRONUNCIATIONS	
Clatskanie	KLAT-ska-nye
Sauvie Island	SO-vee
Vernonia	ver-KNOWN-ya
Scappoose	skah-POOSE

Columbia County is named for the Columbia River. Captain
Robert Gray, in the American vessel *Columbia Rediviva,* on
May 11, 1792 at 8:00 a.m. sailed through the breakers and
sailed upriver.
Source: *Oregon Geographic Names*

THE COLUMBIA RIVER, which forms the north and eastern border
of Columbia county, is arguably the most significant environmental force in the Pacific Northwest region of the United States.
It flows for more than 1,200 miles, from the base of the Canadian
Rockies in southeastern British Columbia to the Pacific Ocean at
Astoria, Oregon. Although humans have lived along the river for
more than 10,000 years, modern engineering in the 19th and 20th
centuries has dramatically altered the Columbia.

JEWELL MEADOWS, in the coast range, has 1,200 acres where a
herd of 200 Roosevelt elk congregate in meadows from December
to February. The staff offers daily, one-hour tours to feed the elk
during this period.

THE COLUMBIA RIVER

"After serving as telegraph operator for a year, father decided to take up outdoor work, so he worked as a bricklayer till 1852, at which time he started across the plains for California. While crossing the plains he heard such favorable reports of Oregon that he changed his destination and came to Oregon City."

– CHARLES L. CONYERS, OF THE PIONEER CONYERS FAMILY OF CLATSKANIE
Source: www.twrps.com

"Oregon was large and had but few people in it. But as the population increases and the valley of the Columbia settles up, the natural good points of St. Helens and Columbia County will come out, and we shall have a handsome and thriving town here yet."

– H. C. VICTOR, ST. HELENS BUSINESSMAN, 1865
Source: www.twrps.com

Coos

COUNTY SEAT: Courthouse,
250 N Baxter, Coquille 97423
PHONE: 541-396-3121, ext. 241
WEB: www.co.coos.or.us
ESTABLISHED: Dec. 22, 1853
ELEV. AT COQUILLE: 40'
AREA: 1,629 sq. mi.
AVERAGE TEMP.: Jan. 44.2°, July 60.9°
ANNUAL PRECIPITATION: 56.8"

ECONOMY: Forest products, fishing, agriculture, shipping, recreation, and tourism.
POINTS OF INTEREST: Lumber port, myrtlewood groves, Oregon Dunes National Recreation Area.

GEOGRAPHIC PRONUNCIATIONS	
Arago	AIR-a-go
Coquille	ko-KEEL

AN AUGUST MORNING ON COOS BAY

STEAM RISES from the shimmering silver glass of the Bay. Above, the brilliant sun prepares her face for the day, surrounding it with diamond facets suffused by a gauzy veil. Her diffused brilliance merges momentarily into pale blue sky.

Delivery trucks and cars begin to rush the stoplights on Highway 101 with the sound of their engines and brakes. In another hour, the town will be alive. I am in a hurry to be at task, talking to people and deciphering words on paper.

Far out in the Bay a lone tug heads slowly seaward. Lapping water, new warmth, an emerald shoreline, and to the west a bustling small city as the sun slowly slips off its veil to reveal a dazzling face. This day, the tug understands a little of eternity.

— CRYSTAL SHOJI, COOS BAY

"I love driving the back roads of Oregon looking at beautiful and clean countryside."

— TIM FRANCE, POWERS

THE OREGON DUNES NATIONAL RECREATION AREA

THE OREGON Dunes National Recreation Area is the largest expanse of coastal sand dunes in the United States. For nearly fifty miles, from the mouth of the Siuslaw, to Cape Blanco at Coos Bay, the largest area of dunes in the country lies between the Pacific Ocean and the Coast Mountains. In places, the dunes extend 2.5 miles inland, and some are as high as 500 feet. In 1972, 32,186 acres of dunes, forest, streams, and lakes were set aside as the Oregon Dunes National Recreation Area.

The unique feature of the Oregon Dunes National Recreation Area is sand! Most of the sand was carried here by the Umpqua River over millions of years. Forests camouflage the underlying sand and few people realize it supports the highways and houses in this area. Spanning 40 miles of the Oregon coastline, dunes surround lakes, forests, and wetlands from Florence to Coos Bay, Oregon.

Source: www.fs.fed.us/r6/siuslaw/oregondunes/

THE OREGON DUNES RECREATIONAL AREA
Miles and miles of picturesque sand dunes blanket the Central Oregon coast.

"There are few things in nature that can match a dune
in grace of curve and contour and in play of light and shadow."
— *A Century of Coos and Curry*, WILLIAM S. COOPER

Crook

COUNTY SEAT: Courthouse,
300 NE 3rd, Prineville 97754
PHONE: 541-447-6553
ESTABLISHED: Oct. 24, 1882
ELEV. AT PRINEVILLE: 2,868'
AREA: 2,991 sq. mi.
AVERAGE TEMP.: Jan. 31.8°, July 64.5°
ANNUAL PRECIPITATION: 10.50"
ECONOMY: Livestock, forest products, recreation, agriculture, manufacturing, and wholesale trade.

POINTS OF INTEREST: Crooked River Canyon, Ochoco Mountains, Prineville and Ochoco Reservoirs, geological formations.

GEOGRAPHIC PRONUNCIATIONS	
Paulina	paw-LYE-na
Ochoco Creek	O-chuh-ko

THREE SCORE have I lived
In this pleasant, high desert;
A native Oregonian
That makes me to be!
And of all of my travels...
Europe, and the Orient,
Finer forests, valleys, deserts
I have YET to see!
There is nothing
So tenacious
As a fierce, life-long Oregonian;
You've only to ask them;
They'll tell you, I'm sure
That if this is God's footstool
How great must His throne be.
We're here to protect it,
And make sure it's secure.

PATRICIA RECK, REDMOND

OCHOCO MOUNTAINS, SUMMIT PRAIRIE
Wildflowers and ponderosa pines

PRINEVILLE is known as the Rockhound Capital of the World for good reason. Hundreds of tourists descend on Crook County every year to prospect at one of the 10 publicly accessible rockhound claims maintained by the chamber of commerce. The thunderegg is the state rock of Oregon (although not technically a rock).
Source: www.naturenw.org

"Home is a place that makes you feel good and gives you what you need. Crisp air, environmental diversity, and good people are a few of the many things that makes Crook County home."

— ROB BONNER, POWELL BUTTE

Curry

COUNTY SEAT: 29821 Ellensburg Ave.,
Gold Beach 97444
PHONE: 541-247-7011, ext. 210
ESTABLISHED: Dec. 18, 1855
ELEV. AT GOLD BEACH: 60'
AREA: 1,648 sq. mi.
AVERAGE TEMP.: Jan. 45.0°, July 65.0°
ANNUAL PRECIPITATION: 82.67"
ECONOMY: Forest products, agriculture,
commercial and sport fishing, recreation,
and tourism.

POINTS OF INTEREST: Cape Blanco
Lighthouse, Rogue River Japanese
Bomb Site.

GEOGRAPHIC PRONUNCIATIONS	
Ophir	O-fuhr
Nesika Beach	nuh-SEE-ka
Langlois	LANG-loy

EASTER LILIES

TODAY OVER 95 percent of all bulbs grown for the potted
Easter Lily market are produced by just ten farms in a narrow
coastal region straddling the California-Oregon border, from
Smith River, California up to Brookings, Oregon.

About 11.5 million Easter Lily bulbs were shipped to
commercial greenhouses in the United States and Canada
in 1996. The Harbor-Brookings region of Southwest Curry
County, Oregon, is known as the Easter Lily Capital of the
World. Here, lily growers toil year-round in their fields to
produce nearly all the bulbs from which the large trumpet-
shaped flowers bloom.

Source: aggie-horticulture.tamu.edu

ROGUE RIVER; A boating party relaxes at a swimming hole on the Rogue between Grants Pass and Gold Beach.

"Landing a beautiful Rogue River Chinook salmon, drinking in the view from a 3,000-foot mountain just minutes from the beach, walking on a pristine beach with no one in sight, not fighting bumper to bumper traffic—these are just a few reasons to love the South Coast.

'There's nothing to do here' has been the complaint of teenagers from time immemorial from every section of the country. True, the mall is not next-door and some South Coasties may have to drive a few miles to a movie, skating rink, bowling alley, or skateboard park. But little theater groups put on some great plays all through the year. And natural opportunities abound. Hiking, boating, water skiing, windsurfing, white water rafting, backpacking, horseback riding, whale watching, crabbing, clam digging, beachcombing, and local community celebrations, etc., provide plenty of opportunities for wholesome and healthful recreation. The air is fresh from the sea.

Yes, the South Coast is far from the bustle of the big cities of the Willamette Valley, but most of us who live here like it that way."

— WALT SCHROEDER, GOLD BEACH

CAPE BLANCO LIGHTHOUSE

Oregon's Most Westerly, Oldest and Highest above the Sea

LISTED ON THE NATIONAL REGISTER OF HISTORIC PLACES

ON THE eve of December 20, 1870, Cape Blanco's Fresnel lens was lit for the first time. H. Burnap hired on as the first keeper of Oregon's most westerly lighthouse. Cape Blanco is also recorded as being the highest above the sea at 245 feet, the oldest continuously operating light, and in 1903, Oregon's first official woman keeper Mable E. Bretherton signed on.

Cape Blanco's history is full of shipwrecks and lives saved. One notable shipwreck was the "J.A. Chanslor" (an oil tanker) in 1919. Of the 39 passengers, only three survived the collision with an offshore rock.

James Langlois and James Hughes were Cape Blanco's most distinguished keepers. (Hughes was the second son of Patrick and Jane Hughes, whose 2,000-acre ranch bordered the Light Station property.) They both served their entire careers at Cape Blanco, Langlois 42 years and Hughes 38 years. Their job included keeping the light working from sunset to sunrise.

Source: www.portorfordoregon.com/blanco.html

Oregon's Lighthouses from South to North

CAPE BLANCO LIGHTHOUSE
COQUILLE RIVER LIGHTHOUSE
CAPE ARAGO LIGHTHOUSE
UMPQUA RIVER LIGHTHOUSE
HECETA HEAD LIGHTHOUSE
YAQUINA BAY LIGHTHOUSE
YAQUINA HEAD LIGHTHOUSE
CAPE MEARES LIGHTHOUSE
TILLAMOOK ROCK LIGHTHOUSE

◄ **CAPE BLANCO LIGHTHOUSE**

The historical Cape Blanco Lighthouse stands on a flower-strewn knoll overlooking the Pacific, warning passing ships away from treacherous waters and cliffs of the Cape.

Deschutes

COUNTY SEAT: Administration Building, 1130 NW Harriman, Bend 97701-1947

PHONE: 541-388-6549

WEB: www.deschutes.org

ESTABLISHED: Dec. 13, 1916

ELEV. AT BEND: 3,628'

AREA: 3,055 sq. mi.

AVERAGE TEMP.: Jan. 30.5°, July 65.5°

ANNUAL PRECIPITATION: 12"

ECONOMY: Tourism, retail trade, forest products, recreational equipment, aviation, software, and high technology.

POINTS OF INTEREST: Mt. Bachelor ski area, Cascade Lakes Highway, Lava River Caves, Lava Cast Forests, Newberry Crater, Smith Rock State Park, Three Sisters Wilderness, Pine Mountain Observatory.

GEOGRAPHIC PRONUNCIATIONS	
Wickiup	WI-kee-uhp
Terrebonne	TEAR-a-bon
Metolius River	met-O-lee-uhs

SMITH ROCK STATE PARK

Basaltic lava flows from Newberry Volcano flowed down the canyon of the Crooked River about 1.2 million years ago. These flows now form low cliffs above the Crooked River in Smith Rock State Park.

THREE SISTERS WILDERNESS

Long before this area was designated as a wilderness, tribes of Native Americans roamed the forests and meadows around the Three Sisters. They gathered huckleberries and venison and obsidian from which they made arrow and spear heads.

NEWBERRY CRATER NATIONAL MONUMENT
Paulina Lake and East Lake, nestled by trees in the Deschutes National Forest.

"Central Oregon is framed by the stunning Cascades Mountains to our west, and miles of wild and unruly high desert scrub to our east. Sun sets over the striking peaks of Mt. Bachelor, the Three Sisters, and Broken Top, just outside our city, where one can hike, bike, or sit on a restaurant deck and simply muse. Running through Bend is the Deschutes River, calling people to our many parks (for more civilized affairs); to our river trails (for wilder experiences); and to wild and scenic stretches just outside the city (where rapids offer true and glorious mayhem for kayakers and fly fishers). This is a community held together through a tremendous sense of caring and involvement and a shared desire to live in one of the most extraordinarily beautiful patches of land on earth."

– KYLA MERWIN, BEND

(91)

Douglas

COUNTY SEAT: Courthouse,
1036 SE Douglas, Rm. 217,
Roseburg 97470
PHONE: 541-440-4323
WEB: www.co.douglas.or.us
ESTABLISHED: Jan. 7, 1852
ELEV. AT ROSEBURG: 479'
AREA: 5,071 sq. mi.
AVERAGE TEMP.: Jan. 41.2°, July 68.4°
ANNUAL PRECIPITATION: 33.35"

ECONOMY: Forest products, mining, agriculture, fishing, and recreation.
POINTS OF INTEREST: Oregon Dunes National Recreation Area, Diamond Lake, historic Oakland, Wildlife Safari.

GEOGRAPHIC PRONUNCIATIONS	
Umpqua	UHMP-kwah
Calapooya Mts.	kal-uh-POO-yuh

OAKLAND

Applegate Trail emigrants included Rev. Joseph A. Cornwall and his family who reached this valley in 1846. Exhausted by the arduous trip, the family built a cabin and endured the winter, moving on north in the spring. Construction of the Oregon & California Railroad caused the relocation and founding of a new town by Alonzo F. Brown in 1872.

Oakland is a unique and charming little town in southwestern Oregon just two miles off Interstate 5. The two block business district consists of the original brick buildings built in the 1890s. Stearns Hardware, for example, has served this community since 1887. More than 80 properties here were constructed between 1852 and 1890.
Source: www.makewebs.com/oakland/history.htm

WINSTON WILDLIFE SAFARI

Experience Oregon's only drive-through park where hundreds of exotic animals from around the world roam free. Discover a photographer's paradise on our 600-acre reserve. Uncaged animals, living much as they would in their natural habitat, are likely to be found anywhere. There are more than 500 animals representing over 80 different species. Source: www.rosenet.net/tourism/wildlife_safari.html

"OREGON IS special because the people of this great state have an appreciation for both the old and the new. While community growth, development, and new things are not necessarily bad, it is Oregon's historic and natural things that have certain intrinsic values due to their function in time and place. Oregonians preserve sites and structures which reflect elements of our local or national history. We have also found win-win solutions by finding worthwhile and beneficial contemporary uses for important old things.

Many Oregonians have a personal ethic which tells them to preserve the spirit of our special places. They do this by keeping our towns and natural areas aesthetically pleasing, fostering civic pride, attracting tourists, encouraging industry, attracting small businesses to our historic districts, strengthening local economies, building appreciation for local history, and creating a greater sense of community by showing a continuity and link between generations.

Within Oregon, I've noticed that good stewardship begins at the local level with strong leadership, vision, collaborative partnership development, and volunteerism. Oregonians work together to safeguard our natural and cultural heritage so that they are available for future generations to enjoy."

— JOE ROSS, ROSEBURG

DIAMOND LAKE

Bordered on the east by Mt. Thielsen at 9,184 feet, and on the west by Mt. Bailey at 8,363 feet, the Diamond Lake area is popular for winter and summer sports, including camping, fishing, hiking, water sports, and cross-country skiing.

Gilliam

COUNTY SEAT: Courthouse,
221 S Oregon St., PO Box 427,
Condon 97823-0427
PHONE: 541-384-2311
ESTABLISHED: Feb. 25, 1885
ELEV. AT CONDON: 2,844'
AREA: 1,223 sq. mi.
AVERAGE TEMP.: Jan. 31.9°, July 71.3°
ANNUAL PRECIPITATION: 11.39"
ECONOMY: Agriculture, recreation,
and environmental services.

POINTS OF INTEREST: Old Oregon
Trail, Lonerock area, Condon historic
district, Native pictographs.

GEOGRAPHIC PRONUNCIATIONS	
Gilliam	GIL-ee-uhm
Condon	KAHN-duhn
Olex	O-leks

ON OREGON'S western edge, never ending waves come ashore in never ending variation. In her mountains snow falls in swirls and drifts into patterns as countless as the snowflakes themselves. Branches of trees are tossed, showing glimpses of mighty trunks clothed in an armor of bark. In all the beautiful variety of nature, does any surpass the hills now softly rounded, now dropping steeply away, covered with grains and inset with the scrub of this part of the land? Winds off the plains chase the young stems, turning them so they show off in wide swaths, a gentle kaleidoscope swirling up the hills.

— JAN MCGOWAN, HILLSBORO

The **COLUMBIA RIVER** provides the perfect backdrop for a local park in Arlington.

"Characteristic of this region are the alternate stretches of growing wheat and fallow land which in early summer resembles a vast checker board of tawny grain and dark, harrowed earth."

– DESCRIPTION OF THE REGION PUBLISHED IN THE 1940 *WPA Guide*

"We don't have enough moisture to argue about it"

– CONDON RESIDENT ON THE ANNUAL RAINFALL, *Roadside History of Oregon*

Grant

COUNTY SEAT: Courthouse,
201 S Humbolt, Canyon City 97820
PHONE: 541-575-1675
WEB: www.grantcounty.cc
ESTABLISHED: Oct. 14, 1864
ELEV. AT CANYON CITY: 3,194'
AREA: 4,528 sq. mi.
AVERAGE TEMP.: Jan. 30.7°, July 68.4°
ANNUAL PRECIPITATION: 14.28"
ECONOMY: Forest products, agriculture, hunting, livestock, and recreation.

POINTS OF INTEREST: John Day Fossil Beds National Monument, Kam Wah Chung Museum, Sacred Totem Pole, Sumpter Valley Railroad, Strawberry Mountain Wilderness, and North Fork John Day River Wilderness.

GEOGRAPHIC PRONUNCIATIONS	
Seneca	SEN-uh-kuh
Silvies	SIL-veez
Galena	gah-LEE-nuh

Grant County contains the headwaters of the John Day River, which has more miles of Wild and Scenic designation than any other river in the United States. More than 60 percent of the land in the county is in public ownership.

The discovery of gold in Canyon Creek in June, 1862 was the beginning of an era which saw $26,000,000 in gold mined from the Canyon City-John Day area. Hundreds of Chinese immigrated to this area during the gold rush to work in the mines. The 1879 Census lists 960 whites and 2,468 Chinese miners in the gold fields of Eastern Oregon. While most were shunned by the white community, a few of the Chinese were accepted.

Among these were "Doc" Ing Hay and Lung On, owners of the Kam Wah Chung & Co. in John Day. The two men provided the community with staples and supplies, and a meeting place in which the local Chinese could worship, smoke opium, talk, and gamble. Doc Hay was an herbalist who treated both whites and Chinese for many years.

Source: www.grantcounty.cc

JOHN DAY FOSSIL BEDS NATIONAL MONUMENT; John Day River passes below Sheep Rock.

JOHN DAY FOSSIL BEDS NATIONAL MONUMENT, PAINTED HILLS
Wildflowers *(Chaenactis nevii)* on desert floor

Harney

COUNTY SEAT: Courthouse,
450 N Buena Vista, Burns 97720
PHONE: 541-573-6641
WEB: www.harneycounty.com
ESTABLISHED: Feb. 25, 1889
ELEV. AT BURNS: 4,148'
AREA: 10,228 sq. mi.
AVERAGE TEMP.: Jan. 27.5°, July 69.4°
ANNUAL PRECIPITATION: 10.13"
ECONOMY: Forest products, manufacturing, livestock, and agriculture.

POINTS OF INTEREST: Steens Mountain, Malheur Cave, Malheur Wildlife Refuge, Alvord Desert and Lake, "P" Ranch Round Barn.

GEOGRAPHIC PRONUNCIATIONS	
Kiger Gorge	KY-ger
Malheur	mahl-yer

The refuge was established by Executive Order of President Theodore Roosevelt in 1908 as a "preserve and breeding ground for native birds." The lands now managed as MALHEUR WILDLIFE REFUGE have been used by humans for over 10,000 years. More than 320 species of birds, 58 species of mammals, 10 species of native fish, five non-native fish species, and a number of reptiles can be found on the 187,000 acres of the refuge during the year.

STEENS MOUNTAIN juts up a mile above the Southeast Oregon desert. The massive fault block mountain is the largest such geologic formation in North America.

STEENS MOUNTAIN under spring snow; county highway near **ALVORD RANCH,** Harney County.

HISTORIC HARNEY, once the county seat, now a ghost town.

"Fall in Harney County is my favorite time of year. What a treat to hear the first honking choruses of geese making their vee-shaped exodus south. The aspen groves on Steens Mountain display their fall wardrobe of brilliant reds, oranges, and yellows as herds of antelope and elk lazily graze next to irrigation pivots in ranch pastures. Harney County winters are also a favorite of mine. The sage and juniper draped in coats of snow, stand like sentinels in the desert fields. The peaceful scene of great red trunks of ponderosa rising up from the snowy white floor of the Malheur Forest is enhanced only by the running water lullaby of Rattlesnake Creek. Spring awakens as the crocus, tulips, and daffodils peek from beneath the thawing ground. Birders come from around the country to visit the Malheur Wildlife Refuge to watch the aerial dance of snow geese, swans, and varieties of ducks. Rain showers and brilliant rainbows add delight to a drive across the desert.

Harney County is the best place to be in the summer. Mann Lake is a favorite fishing hole that yields not only tasty trout, but diverse scenery. From the Alvord Desert to the east rim of Steens Mountain, wildflowers and wildlife abound. The summer comes to an end with the Harney County Fair...food, 4H-ers, rodeo, exhibits, and Harney County folk...then I look forward to fall."

– DONA JOHNSON, BURNS

Hood River

COUNTY SEAT: Courthouse, 309 State St., Hood River 97031-2093
PHONE: 541-386-1442
EMAIL: boc@admin.co.hood-river.or.us
ESTABLISHED: June 23, 1908
ELEV. AT HOOD RIVER: 154'
AREA: 533 sq. mi.
AVERAGE TEMP.: Jan. 33.6°, July 72°
ANNUAL PRECIPITATION: 30.85"

ECONOMY: Fruit orchards, windsurfing
POINTS OF INTEREST: Bridge of the Gods, Cloud Cap Inn, Mt. Hood Recreation Area, Mt. Hood Meadows Ski Resort, Lost Lake, Panorama Point, Hood River Valley at blossom time.

GEOGRAPHIC PRONUNCIATIONS	
Odell	o-DEL

Hood River County is one of the most magnificent and prolific fruit producing valleys in the world. Nationally, it's one of the largest Anjou pear growing districts producing over 50 percent of the nation's winter pears (Anjou, Bosc, Comice). The county produces over 11 percent of all the Bartlett pears grown in the U.S. and the Newtown Pippin apple is considered the highest quality Pippin grown anywhere in the world.

The area's first fruit trees were planted in 1854, when Nathaniel Coe arrived to establish Oregon's first post offices and mail routes. Twenty-two years later, in 1876, E.L. Smith planted the first commercial orchard, consisting of 30 acres of Newtown Pippin and Spitzenburg apples and peaches. In time, apples became the dominant crop. In 1839, the Hood River Valley had a disastrous freeze that killed many apple trees. At that time, many growers replaced their crops with pears, and today pears represent 75 percent of the fruit grown.

What makes the fruit so exceptional is the fertile volcanic soil, produced eons ago by eruptions of long-silent Mt. Hood. Tempered with centuries of decomposed organic materials this mineral rich earth combined with pure glacier water, cool nights, and warm growing days, makes biting into Hood River fruit a crispy, juicy, delicious experience. Source: www.hoodriverfruitloop.com/history.htm

MT. HOOD; Highest peak in the Oregon Cascades; pear orchards in **HOOD RIVER VALLEY.**

"The beauty of this place is like no other. Overlooking the mighty Columbia River, Mt. Hood rises above the fruitful Hood River Valley as our watchful guardian. Wind pushes white caps up out of the raging river into fine mist just above the surface. Sun opens the clouds to reveal mountains in their snowy white robes. Trees laden with the fruits of the season blanket the valley and promise new life upon the return of Spring. People with a dream for this place—dreams of how it used to be, dreams of what it will become—have found refuge within our human community. Forests and rivers, wildlife and wonder! There is no place I would rather be. And when I am here...I am home!"

— KRISTIN M. REESE, HOOD RIVER

Jackson

COUNTY SEAT: Courthouse,
10 S Oakdale, Medford 97501
PHONE: 541-774-6147
WEB: www.jacksoncounty.org
ESTABLISHED: Jan. 12, 1852
ELEV. AT MEDFORD: 1,382'
AREA: 2,801 sq. mi.
AVERAGE TEMP.: Jan. 37.6°, July 72.5°
ANNUAL PRECIPITATION: 19.84"

ECONOMY: Medical, retail, tourism, agriculture, manufacturing, and forest products.
POINTS OF INTEREST: Mt. Ashland Ski Resort, Historic Jacksonville, Shakespearean Festival, Crater Lake Highway.

GEOGRAPHIC PRONUNCIATIONS	
Rogue River	ROAG
Siskiyou	SIS-key-you

Named for President Andrew Jackson, Jackson County was formed in 1852 from Lane County and an area south of Douglas and Umpqua Counties. The discovery of gold near Jacksonville in 1852 and completion of a wagon road, which joined the county with California to the south and Douglas County to the north, brought many pioneers.

JACKSONVILLE

Nestled in the beautiful foothills of the Siskiyou Mountains lies the city of Jacksonville, Oregon. It has long been hailed as one of the most historically significant communities in the western United States. Gold was first discovered in the Oregon Territory at Rich Gulch in 1851. A thriving mining camp emerged along the gold-lined creekbeds and before long, the bustling camp was transformed into a town named "Jacksonville."

Peter Britt, Oregon's first photographer, arrived by oxcart in 1852. After a brief period of gold mining and operating a pack train, he returned to his passion for photography. Britt captured the landscape of Jacksonville's early history with pictures of people, architecture, events, and natural settings that reflected the unusual lives and colorful legends of the day.

Source: www.jacksonvilleoregon.org

JACKSONVILLE MUSEUM, occupying the courthouse built in 1884.

LITHIA PARK, ASHLAND

JOSEPH P. STEWART STATE PARK

OREGON SHAKESPEARE FESTIVAL

The Oregon Shakespeare Festival was established in 1935, in Ashland. In 2000, season attendance exceeded 380,000. The ten millionth ticket holder was welcomed in 2001.

The Festival is among the oldest and largest professional regional repertory theaters in the country. It presents an eight-month season of 11 plays—five by Shakespeare and six by contemporary playwrights.

"Rivers are as important as land, and infinitely more capable of interesting travelers, tourists, and anglers."

- The North Umpqua, Oregon, ZANE GREY

"Medford and the beautiful Rogue Valley is a place blessed with many treasures. From its skilled workforce and beautiful parks, to vibrant economy and cultural offerings, there is something that will draw you in. Maybe it's the rich history of the community, ancestors like Peter Britt, Angus Bowmer, Glenn Jackson, William Smullen, and Otto Frohnmeyer or the industries that are key parts of the Medford/Jackson County economy.

Medford's natural beauty mixes with its strong corporate climate to make it a favorable place to plant roots. That's why people from around the world have come to call this place home. Whether you have lived here one month or all of your life, you can easily understand the reasons why we call Medford 'The Center of it All.' Nestled snugly and conveniently between Portland and San Francisco, this 'Center of it All' is regularly recognized as among the best places to live in the nation."

— BRAD HICKS, MEDFORD

"I love the view from Table Rock in Jackson County. I just love Jackson County."

— MARILYN WEBSTER, SALEM

Jefferson

COUNTY SEAT: 75 SE 'C' St.,
Madras 97741
PHONE: 541-475-4451
ESTABLISHED: Dec. 12, 1914
ELEV. AT MADRAS: 2,242'
AREA: 1,791 sq. mi.
AVERAGE TEMP.: Jan. 37.4°, July 70.1°
ANNUAL PRECIPITATION: 10.2"
ECONOMY: Agriculture, forest products,
and recreation.

POINTS OF INTEREST: Mt. Jefferson,
Warm Springs Indian Reservation,
Santiam Summit, Priday Agate Beds.

GEOGRAPHIC PRONUNCIATIONS	
Madras	MAD-ruhs
Metolius River	met-O-lee-uhs

"A spectacular 50 mile, 360 degree view; Mt. Hood to the north
(ski run lighting the night sky), Mt. Bachelor to the south, the
rest of the snow capped Cascade Mountain Range from the south
circling to the west and vistas of thousands of acres of high desert
rims and plateaus to the east. The most beautiful sunsets in the
northwest often times enjoyed to the tune of the coyote howling
his evening song. Water so pure and tasty that it is bottled and
shipped throughout the United States. Sunshine at least 345 days
a year viewed through some of the cleanest air in Oregon. A smor-
gasbord of wildlife from deer and elk wandering through your
yard to the more exotic bald and golden eagles perched high in
juniper trees watching for their next meal, or the call of the red-
tailed hawk as he circles above, covies of quail roosting in your
trees, lizards scurrying about. We have it all in Central Oregon."

– MARI WYMORE, MADRAS

PONDEROSA PINE GROVE; Central Oregon

"As a native Central Oregonian, I will never tire of the breathtaking beauty of our area, and Jefferson County in particular. Breaking over Juniper Butte while heading north on Highway 97, you will see a beautiful patchwork quilt of fields. The backdrop for this splendid area of the high desert are the Cascade Mountains. Nine of her peaks stand majestic and stunning and are the center of many gorgeous sunsets. The choices of recreation here are as bountiful as the sunshine. Boating, water skiing, fishing, hunting, rock hounding, snow skiing, hiking, and so much more are within a moment's drive. Much like the fields of flowers, grass, crops, and the rich soils of Mother Earth, our people are just as diverse and wonderful. We still hold the small town friendly atmosphere where neighbors help neighbors, and you visit with your friends on the street corners. Jefferson County is home to people of many different ethnic backgrounds. We are a county of color in so many ways, and all the better for it."

— JANET BROWN, MADRAS

Josephine

COUNTY SEAT: Courthouse,
500 NW 6th St., Grants Pass 97526

PHONE: 541-474-5243

WEB: www.co.josephine.or.us

ESTABLISHED: Jan. 22, 1856

ELEV. AT GRANTS PASS: 948'

AREA: 1,641 sq. mi.

AVERAGE TEMP.: Jan. 39.9°, July 71.6°

ANNUAL PRECIPITATION: 32.31"

ECONOMY: Tourism, recreation, forest products, electronics, and software.

POINTS OF INTEREST: Oregon Caves National Monument, Wolf Creek Tavern, Sunny Valley Covered Bridge and Interpretive Center, Kalmiopsis Wilderness.

GEOGRAPHIC PRONUNCIATIONS	
Kalmiopsis	CAL-me-op-sis
Takilma	tuh-KIL-ma

In the spring of 1851, Lloyd Rollins and a party of prospectors, including his teenaged daughter Josephine, were headed for the California gold fields. Upon arriving on the Rogue River, some friendly Indians told them of gold in what later became the Illinois Valley.

Josephine later wrote that it took a week of packing out a road in some places to get within three miles of their destination. They packed into a tributary of the main river, later named Josephine Creek in her honor. Here they indeed found considerable gold.

Source: www.webtrail.com/jchs/history.html

"...the river tumbled off the mountain in mellow thundering music, to meet its main branch, and proud with added strength and beauty, it raced away between its timbered banks down the miles to the sheltered valley...and skirting Grant's Pass, the river twisted and chafed and fought its way through Hell Gate...it entered the canyoned wilderness of the Coast range."

– ZANE GREY, DESCRIPTION OF THE ROGUE RIVER, *Rogue River Feud*, 1929

WHAT MAKES OREGON SPECIAL AND WORTH PRESERVING? "A neighborly mix of strong opinions and values across the whole spectrum."

– AMY WILSON, GRANTS PASS

GRAVE CREEK COVERED BRIDGE
Built in 1920, this is the last covered bridge on the North-South Pacific Hwy.

OREGON CAVES NATIONAL MONUMENT

In 1909, President William Howard Taft proclaimed a tract of 480 acres as Oregon Caves National Monument. Oregon Caves National Monument is rich in diversity. Above ground, the monument encompasses a remnant old-growth coniferous forest. It harbors a fantastic array of plants, and a Douglas fir tree with the widest known girth in Oregon. Below ground is an active marble cave created by natural forces over hundreds of thousands of years in one of the world's most diverse geologic realms.

Source: www.oregoncaves.org

"Colored stalactites seem to drip from the rocky roofs, stalagmites rise off the damp floors, and eerily shaped formations of 'cave popcorn' and 'moonmilk' line the passages."

– DESCRIPTION OF THE OREGON CAVES NATIONAL MONUMENT, www.csaa.com

KALMIOPSIS WILDERNESS

The 180,000-acre Kalmiopsis Wilderness is characterized by deep rough canyons, sharp rock ridges, and clear rushing streams and rivers. The Kalmiopsis represents a unique landscape of unusual beauty composed of diverse topography (elevations from 400 to 5,100 feet), rock, soil, vegetation, and wildlife habitat.

The Kalmiopsis Wilderness is named for a unique shrub, *Kalmiopsis leachiana*, a relic of the pre-ice age and one of the oldest members of the heath *(Ericaceae)* family.

Source: www.fs.fed.us/r6/siskiyou/kalmiop.htm

WOLF CREEK TAVERN

The original hotel was called Six Bit House, and it stood about a mile northeast of the community center. Recent research has shown that the building now known as Wolf Creek Tavern was built around 1883 for Henry Smith, a local merchant-entrepreneur. Wolf Creek Tavern was exceptionally well crafted by local sawyers and skilled workers in the building trades. It served local traffic to area mines and stage travelers connecting between Roseburg and Redding prior to the completion of the Oregon and California railroad through the Siskiyou Mountains in 1887. Wolf Creek Inn is the oldest continuously operated hotel in the Pacific Northwest. It is here that Jack London completed his novel *Valley Of The Moon*. As an important stop on the sixteen day journey from San Francisco to Portland, by stage coach, the Wolf Creek Inn has housed practically every important personage found in the Northwest during the early history of Oregon. Back in the early days of movies, the inn became a refuge for beleaguered actors seeking an escape from the demanding Hollywood studios. Mary Pickford found the inn warm and comforting, especially when Douglas Fairbanks accompanied her on the visit. Clark Gable was a good friend of the innkeeper in the 1930s and stopped by several times while fishing the Rogue River just a few miles west of the inn. Other visitors that have signed the guest register include Carol Lombard and Orson Wells.

Source: www.rogueweb.com/wolfcreekinn

FISHING ON THE ROGUE RIVER ➤

Klamath

COUNTY SEAT: 305 Main St., Klamath Falls 97601-6391

PHONE: 541-883-5134

WEB: www.co.klamath.or.us

ESTABLISHED: Oct. 17, 1882

ELEV. AT KLAMATH FALLS: 4,105'

AREA: 6,135 sq. mi.

AVERAGE TEMP.: Jan. 29.8°, July 68.0°

ANNUAL PRECIPITATION: 14.31"

ECONOMY: Forest products, agriculture, tourism, and recreation.

POINTS OF INTEREST: Crater Lake National Park, Klamath Lake (largest lake in Oregon), seven National Wildlife Refuges.

GEOGRAPHIC PRONUNCIATIONS	
Chemult	SHUH-mult
Chiloquin	CHIL-uh-kwin
Gilchrist	GIL-krist

The legend tells of two Chiefs, Llao of the Below World and Skell of the Above World, pitted in a battle which ended up in the destruction of Llao's home, Mt. Mazama. The battle was witnessed in the eruption of Mt. Mazama and the creation of Crater Lake."
Source: www.nps.gov

"The line recorded the six hundred foot mark, and then eight hundred and nine hundred. Still the lead went down. Something must be wrong with the sounding apparatus...at one thousand two hundred and ten feet it rested on the bottom."

– DESCRIPTION OF THE FIRST OFFICIAL SOUNDING OF CRATER LAKE BY WILLIAM G. STEEL IN AUGUST, 1885.

CRATER LAKE

WHEN PRESIDENT Theodore Roosevelt signed the bill on May 22, 1902 for Crater Lake National Park to become the nation's fifth oldest national park, William Gladstone Steel's dream had become a reality.

Steel, the father of Crater Lake National Park, had been preoccupied with Crater Lake since 1870 when he was a sixteen-year-old boy in Kansas. He learned of Crater Lake when reading a newspaper that was used to wrap his lunch. Two years later he moved to Oregon and in 1885 he and a druggist named John Beck joined a group headed for Crater Lake. When the two men, Steel and Beck finally spotted the lake, the water was so blue it startled them. "All ingenuity of nature seems to have been exerted to the fullest capacity to build a grand awe-inspiring temple the likes of which the world has never seen before," said Steel. His involvement with Crater Lake covered 49 years. After it was made a national park, he realized his work had just begun.

Even before then, Crater Lake was the basis of much local Native American legend, as the stories of its creation have been passed down through the centuries.

The lake was formed after the collapse of an ancient volcano, posthumously named Mount Mazama. This volcano erupted approximately 7,700 years ago. That eruption was 42 times as powerful as the 1980 eruption of Mt. St. Helens. The basin or caldera was formed after the top 5,000 feet of the volcano collapsed. Subsequent lava flows sealed the bottom, allowing the caldera to fill with approximately 4.6 trillion gallons of water from rainfall and snow melt, to create the seventh deepest lake in the world at 1,932 feet.

continued on next page...

Crater Lake continued...

Crater Lake rarely freezes over completely; it last did so in 1949. Heat from the summer sun stored in the immense body of water retards ice formation throughout the winter. On the earth clock, natural forces only recently constructed this landscape. Lava flows first formed a high plateau base on which explosive eruptions then built the Cascade volcanoes.

Shamans in historic time forbade most Indians to view the lake, and Indians said nothing about it to trappers and pioneers, who did not find it for 50 years. Then, in 1853, while searching for the Lost Cabin Gold Mine, some prospectors, including John Wesley Hillman, happened onto Crater Lake. Soundings with piano wire by a U.S. Geological Survey party in 1886 set the lake's depth at 1,996 feet, close to sonar findings of 1,932 feet officially recorded in 1959.

The clean, clear, cold lakewater contained no fish until they were introduced by humans from 1888 to 1941. Today, rainbow trout and kokanee salmon still survive in Crater Lake. Wildflowers bloom late and disappear early here, thriving in wet, open areas. Birds and other animals often seen are ravens, jays, nutcrackers, deer, ground squirrels, and chipmunks. Present but seldom seen are elk, black bear, foxes, porcupines, pine martens, chickaree squirrels, and pikas.

Source: www.crater.lake.national-park.com

◄ **CRATER LAKE NATIONAL PARK, OREGON CASCADES**
An old snag clings to the rim of Crater Lake.

Lake

COUNTY SEAT: Courthouse, 513 Center St., Lakeview 97630

PHONE: 541-947-6006

ESTABLISHED: Oct. 24, 1874

ELEV. AT LAKEVIEW: 4,800'

AREA: 8,359 sq. mi.

AVERAGE TEMP.: Jan. 28.4°, July 67.0°

ANNUAL PRECIPITATION: 15.80"

ECONOMY: Livestock, forest products, agriculture, and recreation.

POINTS OF INTEREST: Hart Mountain Antelope Refuge, Fort Rock, Old Perpetual Geyser, Warner Canyon Ski Area, Lost Forest, Sheldon National Wildlife Refuge, Summer Lake Hot Springs, Hole-in-the-Ground, sunstones (Oregon's state gemstone) near Plush, Warner Wetlands, Summer Lake Wildlife Area.

GEOGRAPHIC PRONUNCIATIONS	
Paisley	PAIZ-lee
Sycan Marsh	SIGH-can

"...known as the Oregon Outback, a land with ruggedness—where life is tied to the land and heritage values, where people seek independence but know each other's first names, and community is paramount."

– JONATHAN NICHOLAS
Source: www.lakecountychamber.org

HART MOUNTAIN

Hart Mountain is a large fault block ridge that is approximately 30 miles to the east of Lakeview. At the base of the mountain lies the Warner Wetlands. This is an ideal place for observing waterfowl and other wildlife. A developed trail leads a half-mile into the wetlands to a bird blind. On the top of the mountain is the Hart Mountain National Antelope Refuge. While the pronghorn antelope make their home on the rolling, sage-covered plains, bighorn sheep are at home along the mountain's ridge.

Source: www.oregonoutback.com

FORT ROCK STATE MONUMENT

FORT ROCK

Fort Rock is a large remnant of a volcano that once rose from the valley floor. It towers 325 feet above the desert floor and is about a half-mile wide.

In 1937, a prehistoric shoe made of sagebrush was discovered in a cave at Fort Rock by a group from Oregon State University.

SUMMER LAKE PETROGLYPHS

FOR THOUSANDS of years Summer Lake has been an important region for humans. Native Americans lived and hunted here while the Ice Age lakes were slowly drying up. Evidence of their reverence for the land abounds in the revealing and well-preserved petroglyphs. The area around Summer Lake is one of the richest in the world for petroglyphs and other evidence of an earlier people who lived here. In the quiet of evening with the purest of skies above, you may hear the echo of ancient folks still ringing in the clear air.

From bluffs near the Chewaucan River to Hart Mountain and all over Lake County, petroglyphs are abundant. Images depicting hunting, wildlife, and many other scenes have been etched into the stone leaving a message for those who come later. The petroglyphs' meanings are sometimes obvious, such as a sheep nursing its kid or lightning and rain descending from a cloud, but often they are a mystery. Why were these enigmatic messages left here? What did they mean to their creators? What do they mean for us?

This mystery transports you into an older time—a time before the white man came to Summer Lake, a time of survival depending upon your own skills. With the sounds of modern wildlife surrounding you and the air as clean and clear as thousands of years ago, pondering these mysteries seems natural. Somehow the connection with the ancient peoples brings a renewed sense of wonder—the majesty of rain, walking across the land, the renewal of life in the spring, and the depth of the sky.

Source: www.summerlakeinn.com

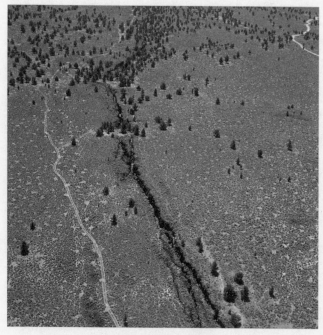

CRACK IN THE GROUND
Christmas Valley, Lake County; 1,000 years or older

HOLE-IN-THE-GROUND

Hole-in-the-Ground is a large crater nearly one mile across and 300 feet deep. Although it closely resembles a crater caused by a meteor strike, it is thought to be the result of volcanic activity simply because it lacks the metal fragments found in meteor strikes.

CRACK-IN-THE-GROUND

Crack-in-the-Ground is a large, deep fissure approximately two miles long and 70 feet deep. It is uncommon for such rifts to remain open, which makes Crack-in-the-Ground an unusual landmark. It is estimated that it has remained open for a thousand years.

Lane

COUNTY SEAT: Courthouse,
125 E 8th, Eugene 97401
PHONE: 541-682-4234
WEB: www.co.lane.or.us
ESTABLISHED: Jan. 28, 1851
ELEV. AT EUGENE: 422'
AREA: 4,620 sq. mi.
AVERAGE TEMP.: Jan. 40°, July 70°
ANNUAL PRECIPITATION: 46"
ECONOMY: Agriculture, higher education, high technology, forest products, recreation, RV manufacturing, and tourism.

POINTS OF INTEREST: Twenty historic covered bridges, coastal sand dunes, Heceta Head Lighthouse, hot springs, McKenzie Pass, sea lion caves, vineyards and wineries, Willamette Pass ski area.

GEOGRAPHIC PRONUNCIATIONS	
Heceta Beach	heh-SEE-tah
Siuslaw River	sigh-YOO-slaw

"...a place where Bach and boot-scootin' live in harmony, where tie-dye and tuxedos are equally trendy, where small town charm meets big-city panache."

Source: www.visitlanecounty.org

SEA LION CAVES

Eleven miles north of Florence, you have it all at Sea Lion Caves: dramatic scenery, wild animals, and the world's largest sea cave. There are special vantage points for spectacular photos and watching for migrating gray whales. Here you see wild, golden, Steller sea lions inside the cave or on the rock ledges outside. In season, there are pigeon guillemot's whistling inside the cave, rhinoceros auklet's and cormorants nesting. And the huge cave, the most beautiful and colorful of sea caves.

Source: www.sealioncaves.com

Beautiful green trees line the banks of the **ROW RIVER** in Lane County.

"I am writing about a very special place for me. I am 34 years old and for approximately 30 years, my family and I have been spending two weeks in the summer at Mercer Lake, located just north of Florence, Oregon. The lake itself is amazingly beautiful! In the still of the mornings, as the fog literally rolls off the lake, the deep water reflects the lush greenness of the surrounding combination of conifer and deciduous trees, ferns, and rhododendrons. The multitude of small, tucked away coves is endless. I have seen many lakes around Oregon. While many of these are beautiful and unique in their own ways, I would have to pick Mercer as the most scenic and peaceful of lakes."

– MICHELLE CARY, PRINEVILLE

Lincoln

COUNTY SEAT: Courthouse,
225 W Olive St., Newport 97365
PHONE: 541-265-4131
WEB: www.co.lincoln.or.us
ESTABLISHED: Feb. 20, 1893
ELEV. AT NEWPORT: 134'
AREA: 992 sq. mi.
AVERAGE TEMP.: Jan. 44.4°, July 57.5°
ANNUAL PRECIPITATION: 71.93"
ECONOMY: Tourism, government,
services/retail, forest products, and fishing.

POINTS OF INTEREST: Alsea Bay
Interpretive Center, Cape Perpetua Visitors'
Center, Cascade Head, OSU Hatfield Marine
Science Center and Interpretive Center,
Oregon Coast Aquarium, Otter Crest
Viewpoint, Seal Rock Park, South Beach
State Park, Yaquina Bay and Lighthouse.

GEOGRAPHIC PRONUNCIATIONS	
Siletz	suh-LETZ
Yachats	YAH-hots
Yaquina	yuh-KWEN-uh

"Living on the coast gives me a link to the uniqueness of the
Oregon spirit. Every time I wander down to Moolack Beach or
out Yaquina Head, I feel connected to the Beach Bill and the
efforts of thousands of Oregonians to make our state a place
we're deeply proud of."

– GUY DITORRICE, NEWPORT

OREGON'S OSU HATFIELD MARINE SCIENCE VISITOR CENTER

Oregon's OSU Hatfield Marine Science Visitor Center creates a
unique, dynamic environment for lifelong exploration and discovery.
The Visitor Center encourages adults and children to enjoy marine
science.

The exhibits and programs explain how scientific research
enhances our ability to interpret the natural patterns that shape our
world and enables us to better appreciate, manage, and sustain
coastal and marine resources.

The Visitor Center is proud to be a Coastal Ecosystem
Learning Center, one of a handful of centers nationwide that
teach, share research, and inform the public about our coastal
and marine habitats. Source: www.hmsc.orst.edu/visitor/vcbasics.html

YAQUINA BAY LIGHTHOUSE

A PIECE of Oregon history sits atop a bluff at the mouth of the Yaquina River. It is the Historic Yaquina Bay Lighthouse, built in 1871 and decommissioned in 1874. It is believed to be the oldest structure in Newport. It is also the only existing Oregon lighthouse with the living quarters attached, and the only historic wooden Oregon lighthouse still standing. The Yaquina Bay Lighthouse is listed in the National Register of Historic Places. The Yaquina Bay Lighthouse has been restored as a working lighthouse and an aid to navigation by the Oregon Parks and Recreation Department, with the help of many people and agencies, including Yaquina Lights, Inc. The official relighting ceremony with the US Coast Guard took place on December 7, 1996. The light shines with a steady white light from dusk to dawn (and sometimes on dark days, because it is controlled by a photocell). The light is 161 feet above sea level.

Source: www.yaquinalights.org

CASCADE HEAD PRESERVE

RISING 1,200 feet above the surf, Cascade Head is one of several coastal promontories formed by the uplift of underwater volcanic basalt flows. Its precipitous cliffs give way to grasslands, alder groves, and a rainforest of spruce and hemlock dripping with lichens, mosses, and ferns. The preserve hosts rare plants, animals, and grassland communities once abundant along the Oregon Coast. It is unusual for the extent of its prairies dominated by native species, including red fescue, wild rye, Pacific reedgrass, Indian paintbrush, prairie rocket, goldenrod, blue violet, and streambank lupine. Three rare species occur on Cascade Head's steep slopes: the Cascade Head catchfly *(Silene douglasii var. oraria)*; hairy checkermallow *(Sidalcea hirtipes)*; and the federally protected Oregon silverspot butterfly *(Speyeria zerene hippolyta)*. Because of its ecological significance, Cascade Head has been designated a State Natural Area, a National Scenic Natural Area, and a United Nations Biosphere Reserve.

The 270-acre preserve is owned by The Nature Conservancy, a non-profit group that protects key habitats and has about 50 nature preserves in Oregon. Cascade Head is managed jointly by the Conservancy and the U.S. Forest Service.

Source: www.nature.org

CASCADE HEAD PRESERVE

This is one of those places where you'd think you'd run into Hansel and Gretel's cottage or come face to face with a tree gnome in the mossy woods.

———

DESCRIPTION OF THE 9,670-ACRE CASCADE HEAD
RESEARCH NATURAL AREA

Linn

COUNTY SEAT: Courthouse,
300 4th Ave. SW,
P.O. Box 100, Albany 97321
PHONE: 541-967-3831
WEB: www.co.linn.or.us
ESTABLISHED: Dec. 28, 1847
ELEV. AT ALBANY: 210'
AREA: 2,297 sq. mi.
AVERAGE TEMP.: Jan. 39.0°, July 65.6°
ANNUAL PRECIPITATION: 42.55"
ECONOMY: Agriculture, forest products,
rare metals, manufacturing, and recreation.

POINTS OF INTEREST: Cascade
Mountain range with Mt. Jefferson,
Hoodoo Ski Bowl and the Pacific
Crest Trail, covered bridges.

GEOGRAPHIC PRONUNCIATIONS	
Calapooia River	kal-uh-POO-yuh
Santiam	san-tee-AM
Scio	SIGH-o

Named after U.S. Senator Lewis F. Linn of Missouri, who was
the author of the Donation Land Act, which provided free land to
settlers in the West.

Linn County is the nation's largest producer of cool season
grass seed crops such as perennial and annual ryegrass. Ryegrass
is commonly used for home lawns, parks, playgrounds, athletic
fields, and golf courses.

PACIFIC CREST TRAIL

The Pacific Crest Trail (PCT) which goes through Linn County is
the jewel in the crown of America's scenic trails, spanning 2,650
miles from Mexico to Canada through three western states. It
reveals the beauty of the desert, unfolds the glaciated expanses
of the Sierra Nevada, and provides commanding vistas of volcanic
peaks and glaciers in the Cascade Range. The trail also passes
through historic mining sites and evidence of man's endless quest
for natural resources. Thousands of hikers and equestrians enjoy
this national treasure each year. Some only travel a few miles,
while others complete every mile in a single season!

Source: www.pcta.org

MT. JEFFERSON from Central Oregon

"I work with Linn County citizens on a variety of water resources issues. The number of community volunteers keeps growing by leaps and bounds! The Girl Scouts love to stencil storm drains with the message that the drains lead straight to our creeks. Some Boy Scouts proudly removed most of an old truck from an Albany creek during a river cleanup. Ten school groups from four schools braved the wettest and windiest weather of the fall to prepare and plant 3,500 willow and dogwood cuttings on a barren stream bank. City of Albany employees and other community members volunteer their time toward all of these projects. Watershed council members work together to protect and restore watershed health in the South Santiam and Calapooia watersheds.

What all of these people have in common is their commitment and connection to the rivers, creeks, wetlands, and landscapes of Linn County. The new City of Albany Natural Resources Advisory Committee recently summarized their goal: 'Protecting what we love about our community.' That message says it all."

– CHERYL HUMMON, WATER RESOURCES PROGRAM COORDINATOR, CITY OF ALBANY

MT. JEFFERSON

MT. JEFFERSON, Oregon's second highest peak at 10,497 feet, is a stratovolcano made of andesite and dacite. It formed during two episodes. The earlier episode constructed a volcano that was probably higher than the present-day Mt. Jefferson. Glaciers carved deep canyons into this volcano. This episode ended with the growth of dacite domes near the summit and collapse of the domes to produce ash flows. The more recent episode of volcanism probably occurred when there were glaciers on Mt. Jefferson. The distribution of the lava flows has an unusual pattern. Instead of spreading out over a large area they are all stacked on top of each other. This pattern was probably caused by the flows being contained in steep glacier valleys. The flows are also very glassy and have unusual joints, features that result from contact with ice. Mt. Jefferson has not erupted in historic time. There is a suspected eruption at South Cinder Peak in 950 A.D. Jefferson erupted in 4,500 B.C. at Forked Butte, south-southeast of the main volcano.

The Mt. Jefferson Wilderness Area is 111,177 acres in size, and has more than 150 lakes to visit.

◅ **MT. JEFFERSON**
Alpine meadows and snow melt lakes punctuate the Mt. Jefferson Wilderness Area.

Malheur

COUNTY SEAT:
251 B Street West, Vale 97918
PHONE: 541-473-5151
WEB: www.malheurco.org
ESTABLISHED: Feb. 17, 1887
ELEV. AT VALE: 2,243'
AREA: 9,926 sq. mi.
AVERAGE TEMP.: Jan. 28.7°, July 75.6°
ANNUAL PRECIPITATION: 9.64"
ECONOMY: Agriculture, livestock, food processing, and recreation.

POINTS OF INTEREST: Oregon Trail, Owyhee Lake, Leslie Gulch Canyon, Jordan Craters, grave of trapper John Baptist Charbonneau, Jordan Valley Basque Pelota Court, the Four Rivers Cultural Center.

GEOGRAPHIC PRONUNCIATIONS	
Juntura	juhn-TUHR-uh
Nyssa	NIS-uh
Owyhee	oh-WHY-hee

MALHEUR COUNTY

Malheur County derives its name from the "Riviere au Malheur" or "Unfortunate River" named by French trappers whose property and furs were stolen from their river encampment.

The county is 94 percent rangeland.

FOUR RIVERS CULTURAL CENTER AND MUSEUM IN ONTARIO

For centuries, the Snake, the Malheur, the Owyhee, and the Payette have supported life. Where the rivers converge and cultures unite this center has been built to serve this community.

JORDAN VALLEY

Jordan Valley is a 19th century Basque community, settled by sheepherders from the Pyrenees Mountains of Spain and France. It is home of Oregon's last remaining fronton, a stone court built in 1915 for playing pelota or handball.

Fantastic rock formations border **LESLIE GULCH**.

"Pioneers heading west departed from Fort Boise following the Oregon Trail northward. Crossing the Malheur River...often stopping long enough to rest and do laundry in the hot springs before heading on their way."

Source: www.malheurco.org

Marion

COUNTY SEAT: Courthouse Square,
555 Court St. NE, Salem 97309-5036
PHONE: 503-588-5225
WEB: www.open.org/~marion
ESTABLISHED: July 5, 1843
ELEV. AT SALEM: 154'
AREA: 1,194 sq. mi.
AVERAGE TEMP.: Jan. 39.3°, July 66.3°
ANNUAL PRECIPITATION: 40.35"
ECONOMY: Government, agriculture,
food processing, forest products,
manufacturing, education, and tourism.

POINTS OF INTEREST: State Capitol,
Champoeg State Park, Silver Falls State
Park, The Oregon Garden, Breitenbush
Hot Springs, Mt. Angel Abbey.

GEOGRAPHIC PRONUNCIATIONS	
Olallie Lakes	o-LAL-ee
Idanha	ee-DAN-uh
Keizer	KEI-zuhr
Champoeg	sham-POO-ee

STATE CAPITOL; Salem

"I'VE CHASED the sun downhill hundreds of times from the eastern tip of Marion County at Mt. Jefferson's base to the county's western edge at the banks of the Willamette. This magical journey traces a cross section of the Willamette watershed. The journey begins where the North Fork of the Santiam River, named for a tribe long gone, begins as rivulets born of snow and ice in enchanted forests. It flows through towns like the one I grew up in that are still adapting to the fact that now big trees are more valuable standing up than lying down. Lower down in Marion County, the canyons open up to the legendary Willamette Valley farmland that produces more farm gate value than any other Oregon county. Again, change, growth and competing uses are revaluing water and raising the question, 'How much can this valley gracefully accommodate?' We are greeted in Salem by the golden pioneer, axe in hand. Maybe he should turn toward the Willamette, whose waters reflect the health of everything uphill or upstream. We're pioneers too, exploring the unfamiliar territory of rapid change, searching for new balance points. We'll do fine; if we look, each day brings fresh awareness of how special this little place is."

— JOHN MILLER, SALEM

"TO THE east the white slopes of Mt. Jefferson begin the day, framed by the rising sun. By dark, rain can be heard knocking on the skylight, the smell of the ocean almost hidden in the downpour. Goose music fills the air, even at night. My dreams take me to my boyhood home in Woodburn, smelling and feeling the fresh-turned earth, ready for planting, and summer air heavy with sweet berries and the clatter of the cannery. I miss the bold crowing of pheasants from fencerows, replaced by streets and houses now. The Willamette flows silently, perhaps more quietly, than before. Still, there is beauty here, and I know I am home."

— BILL HASTIE, SALEM

Morrow

COUNTY SEAT: Courthouse,
100 Court St., Heppner 97836
PHONE: 541-676-5603
E-MAIL: bbloodsworth@co.morrow.or.us
ESTABLISHED: Feb. 16, 1885
ELEV. AT HEPPNER: 1,955'
AREA: 2,049 sq. mi.
AVERAGE TEMP.: Jan. 33.1°, July 69.0°
ANNUAL PRECIPITATION: 12.5"
ECONOMY: Agriculture, food
processing, dairies, utilities, forest
products, livestock, and recreation.

POINTS OF INTEREST: Columbia
River, Blue Mountains, Umatilla
National Forest, Oregon Trail, Blue
Mountain Scenic Byway, Lewis and
Clark Route.

GEOGRAPHIC PRONUNCIATIONS	
Morrow	MAHR-o
Ione	I-own
Lena	LEE-nah

This area is made up of separate "exotic terranes," areas that were created elsewhere and scooped up by North America as it moved west toward the Pacific. Fossils found in this province reveal their foreign origins. Placer and lode gold mines were active here in the past, and...are vivid reminders of the Blue Mountains gold mining heritage.

"Nature stretched her bare and mighty arms around us! The mountains hid the lower sky, and walled about the lower world! We looked upon the beautiful heights of the Blue Mountains, and ate among its spring blossoms, its singing pines, and holy battlements, ten thousand feet above the sea."

– THOMAS JEFFERSON FARNHAM, SEPTEMBER 21, 1839

Source: www.usgennet.org

OREGON TRAIL MARKER; Cecil

MORROW COUNTY MUSEUM

The Morrow County Museum in Heppner, Oregon has one of the finest collections of the artifacts of pioneer, homestead, agricultural, and rural history in the Northwest. The Oregon Trail bisects the County, but the desolate country through which it passes did not slow the pioneers heading for the green Oregon of their dreams. Twenty years later, the burgeoning cities of western Oregon started crowding a few hardy souls who remembered the knee-high grass and solitude through which they had passed. These latter-day Oregon Trail immigrants traveled east on the Trail, bringing families and livestock to wrest a living and establish a culture in a hard and demanding land. Hundreds of photographs in the collection of the Morrow County Museum document the social, economic and technological development of Morrow County. Exhibits range from agricultural history to a discussion of the Native American presence in the county; from the history of rural medical care to the story of the Heppner Flood.

Source: www.mcmuseum.org

Multnomah

COUNTY SEAT: Courthouse, 1021 SW 4th, Portland 97204

PHONE: 503-823-4000

WEB: www.co.multnomah.or.us

ESTABLISHED: Dec. 22, 1854

ELEV. AT PORTLAND: 77'

AREA: 465 sq. mi.

AVERAGE TEMP.: Jan. 38.9°, July 67.7°

ANNUAL PRECIPITATION: 37.39"

ECONOMY: Manufacturing, transportation, wholesale and retail trade, and tourism.

POINTS OF INTEREST: Oregon Historical Center, Oregon Museum of Science and Industry, Washington Park, Oregon Zoo, Rose Test Gardens, Japanese Gardens, Classical Chinese Garden, Multnomah Falls, Oregon Convention Center.

GEOGRAPHIC PRONUNCIATIONS	
Glisan	GLEE-son
Multnomah	muhlt-NO-mu
Wahkeena Falls	wah-KEEN-uh
Oneonta Gorge	o-nee-AHN-tah

"It started to rain. I sat down in a rocking chair next to the stove and looked out the window at the gray, dark, dank rain. Is *this* to be my new life? But the rain was somehow very comforting, and rather than fight it, I decided to go out in it, and embrace the elements.

In the next moment, there stretched across the road on which I was standing, a rainbow. I watched in amazement as it painted itself from left to right, arcing directly over my head, and completing its course in the field to my right. I was standing in the middle of a rainbow! In that moment I knew with absolute certainty, that I was in the most beautiful place in the world. As I tell my East Coast friends when they ask me how I like living in Oregon, 'So. What's not to like?' I have learned the Oregonian way of understatement."

— JAY YOUNG GERARD, PORTLAND

"Having grown up in the eastern US I have lived over 27 years in Oregon which I now consider my home. What stands out for me is the spirit of Oregon's people brought to the Northwest by the original pioneers. Oregonians love their state as is evident by practices and activities that preserve and protect the natural environment."

— CATHY MEYER, PORTLAND

PORTLAND
Mt. Hood in the background

"WHAT I MOST treasure about living in the Portland metropolitan region is the integration of the built and natural environment. When many Oregonians think about nature it is often the coast, the high desert or Cascades that come to mind. For me, even though I love traveling to the Steens, the Alvord, and the Oregon coast, what I find exciting is the knowledge that just a short walk or bicycle ride from home I can see several hundred sandhill cranes dancing in farm fields just outside the Urban Growth Boundary at Sauvie Island; watch nesting great blue herons and bald eagles on Ross Island, in the heart of Portland; explore myriad natural areas along the 160-mile 40-Mile Loop recreational trail system; or see river otter, beaver, and kingfishers from my kayak on the Tualatin River. Our collective efforts to create an urban environment in which access to nature plays a central role in growth management at the regional scale, while creating livable neighborhoods at the local scale, makes this an incredibly exciting time to live in the Portland-Vancouver region."

— MIKE HOUCK, Urban Naturalist for Audubon Society of Portland and chair, Natural Resources Working Group, Coalition for a Livable Future and NW Portland resident

Polk

COUNTY SEAT: Courthouse,
850 Main St., Dallas 97338
PHONE: 503-623-9217
WEB: www.co.polk.or.us
ESTABLISHED: Dec. 22, 1845
ELEV. AT DALLAS: 325'
AREA: 745 sq. mi.
AVERAGE TEMP.: Jan. 39.1°, July 65.6°
ANNUAL PRECIPITATION: 51.66"
ECONOMY: Agriculture, forest products,
manufacturing, electronics, and education.

POINTS OF INTEREST: Western
Oregon University, covered bridges,
Baskett Slough National Wildlife
Refuge, mountain scenery, wineries,
Confederated Tribes of Grand Ronde
Headquarters.

GEOGRAPHIC PRONUNCIATIONS	
Rickreall	rik-ree-AHL
Luckiamute River	LUCK-e-am-yewt
Grand Ronde	rawnd

BASKETT SLOUGH NATIONAL WILDLIFE REFUGE

Baskett Slough National Wildlife Refuge was created to provide
vital wintering habitat for dusky Canada geese. Unlike other
Canada geese, duskies have limited summer and winter ranges.
They nest on Alaska's Copper River Delta and winter almost
exclusively in the Willamette Valley. Habitat loss, predation, and
hunting have caused a decrease in population. The refuge's irri-
gated-farmed fields, rolling oak-covered hills, grass fields, and
shallow wetlands are home to many wildlife species. Several
species of waterfowl, herons, hawks, quail, shorebirds, woodpeck-
ers, and a variety of neotropical birds also frequent the area.

POLK COUNTY VINEYARDS

Polk County pioneers were well-educated, industrious, progressive, law-abiding, and peaceful. This is shown in their participation in making a good government in Oregon, their diligence in clearing land for farming, building permanent homes, establishment of schools and four colleges, industries, etc.

Source: "Historically Speaking," Polk County Historical Society, 1967

Western Oregon University, the oldest college in the Oregon State System of Higher Education, was founded in 1856 by pioneers who crossed the Oregon Trail. Today it continues as a small, comprehensive liberal arts college, offering a well-rounded education to 4,000 students, most of whom are from Oregon.

REFLECTIONS ON POLK COUNTY

"IN ONE of our family's photo albums there are pictures of white-water streams, a flock of geese in an emerald-green field, historic buildings and a pioneer trail, snow covered mountains, people canoeing on a major river, water falls in a rain forest, sweeping valley vistas with volcanic mountain backdrops, a beautifully landscaped university campus, and a trail through an ancient forest. It's hard to make my midwestern friends believe that all of those pictures were taken within a few miles of my Polk County home."

—

"AT A RECENT illegal dumpsite cleanup, deep in the Polk County Coast Range, I looked around and saw that the volunteers included loggers, university professors, storeowners, retired folks, county commissioners, and high school students. I like living in this area because the sense of community clearly includes an unspoken agreement that the place is beautiful and because the good people who want to keep it that way transcend occupations, age, or personal politics."

– JOHN FREEBURG, MONMOUTH

Stately firs line hiking trail in springtime.

Sherman

COUNTY SEAT: Courthouse, 500 Court St., Moro 97039

PHONE: 541-565-3606

ESTABLISHED: Feb. 25, 1889

ELEV. AT MORO: 1,807'

AREA: 831 sq. mi.

AVERAGE TEMP.: Jan. 30.7°, July 67.9°

ANNUAL PRECIPITATION: 9.15"

ECONOMY: Tourism, wheat, barley, and cattle.

POINTS OF INTEREST: John Day Dam, Sherar's Grade, Deschutes State Park.

GEOGRAPHIC PRONUNCIATIONS	
Rufus	ROO-fuhs
Moro	MOR-oh

Sherman County is frequently referred to as the "Land Between the Rivers." Located in north central Oregon, the Columbia River forms the northern border, while the east and west boundaries are marked by the steep, deep canyons of the John Day River on the east and the Deschutes River on the west. The rugged canyons of Buck Hollow, a tributary of the Deschutes, mark the southwest border.

Sherman County is also known as "The Land of Wheat." Encompassing a total of 531,840 acres (831 square miles; approximately 20 miles wide and 42 miles long), nearly 58 percent of the county's land is tilled and soft white winter wheat is the major crop. In fact, Sherman County is annually the third largest wheat-producing county in Oregon, despite being 29th out of 36 counties in size. However, the 58 percent of land tilled ranks number one, far above the state average of 8 percent of tilled land per county. Sherman County is the only county in Oregon without natural forestation.

Source: www.osu.orst.edu/extension/sherman

Ripe wheat ready to harvest.

"Sherman County! Everyone can choose to have a voice in the governance and success of every aspect of our small rural county communities...education, government, and cultural, social and youth organizations. In living here, I appreciate the simple things in life...family, friends and neighbors, rain drops on thirsty soil, grain waving in the wind, great white clouds and blue skies, and small-town business people. Each person can make a difference."

- SHERRY KASEBERG, SHERMAN COUNTY COMMISSIONER AND SHERMAN COUNTY HISTORICAL MUSEUM COORDINATOR

Tillamook

COUNTY SEAT: Courthouse,
201 Laurel Ave., Tillamook 97141
PHONE: 503-842-3402
WEB: www.co.tillamook.or.us
ESTABLISHED: Dec. 15, 1853
ELEV. AT TILLAMOOK: 22'
AREA: 1,125 sq. mi.
AVERAGE TEMP.: Jan. 42.2°, July 58.2°
ANNUAL PRECIPITATION: 90.90"
ECONOMY: Agriculture, forest products, fishing, and recreation.

POINTS OF INTEREST: Neahkahnie Mountain, Nestucca Bay, Pioneer Museum, Tillamook Cheese Factory, Haystack Rock at Cape Kiwanda.

GEOGRAPHIC PRONUNCIATIONS	
Garibaldi	ga-ruh-BAHL-dee
Neahkahnie Mt.	NEE-a-con-nee
Nehalem	nuh-HAIL-luhm
Neskowin	NES-co-win

"I know that much remains to be done, but ahhhhh, the scene from my window today has everything on hold. A train of swells 30 feet high is pounding the rocks and shore, creating a foamy chaos, a roar to match any plane, and a trembling of the earth easy to feel, and all of this highlighted by quick bursts of sunlight between racing clouds. An eagle flew north up the bay, landed on the sandspit to investigate a possible tasty morsel tossed up with the tide, then flew off again. Then a coyote appeared, sniffing through the same piles of storm-tossed debris. These pesky interruptions make getting anything done a joke, and I wouldn't have it any other way!!"

— JIM MUNDELL, NETARTS

THE TILLAMOOK AIR MUSEUM

This museum is housed in a blimp hanger completed in 1943. The building is more than 15 stories in height, and covers more than seven acres (enough to play six football games). It houses the largest collection of flyable warplanes in the Pacific Northwest.

Spruce trees in Oregon's coastal dairyland.

THE TILLAMOOK BURN

The Tillamook Burn was the collective name for a series of wild-fires that struck the northern Oregon Coast Range in the 1930s and 1940s. The fires blackened more than 550 square miles. In the years since the fires, more than 72 million seedlings have been planted by hand across the blackened landscape.

"...perhaps the one place where people would look at a 26-year-old hunk of cheese and reach for a cracker."

– AAA VIA MAGAZINE, www.csaa.com

"The cheese itself appears to be the product of Destiny working with a curious and heroic sort of material, a material of humanity and environment, a material of aspirations and necessities and frustrations."

– "THE CHEDDAR BOX", DEAN COLLINS, 1933

A RESPONSE TO THE QUESTION

"WHY IS OREGON SPECIAL AND WORTH PRESERVING?"

"THE SPIRIT of cooperation and collaboration runs deep among Oregonians. People take care of each other and this type of goodness is building healthy, sustainable communities."

– MAITA BROOKS, TILLAMOOK

"I love to see Oregonians rally each year to clean up our beaches."

– ROGER RADA, TILLAMOOK

"I love the beach at Tierra Del Mar. To have such a beautiful spot that belongs to all of us is an incredible gift."

– MARILYN WALSTER, SALEM

"Oregon is special to me because of the giving spirit of the people who live here."

– ED ARMSTRONG, HEBO

OREGON COAST FROM ATOP NEAHKAHNIE MOUNTAIN ➤

Umatilla

COUNTY SEAT: Courthouse, 216 SE 4th St., Pendleton 97801

PHONE: 541-276-7111

WEB: www.co.umatilla.or.us

ESTABLISHED: Sept. 27, 1862

ELEV. AT PENDLETON: 1,068'

AREA: 3,231 sq. mi.

AVERAGE TEMP.: Jan. 31.9°, July 73.6°

ANNUAL PRECIPITATION: 12.97"

ECONOMY: Agriculture, food processing, forest products, tourism, manufacturing, recreation, aggregate production, and power generation.

POINTS OF INTEREST: Pendleton Round-Up, Pendleton Woolen Mills, Pendleton Underground, North Fork Umatilla Wilderness Area, Tollgate-Spout Springs Recreation Area, Confederated Tribes of the Umatilla Indian Reservation and Tamastslikt Cultural Center.

GEOGRAPHIC PRONUNCIATIONS	
Ukiah	you-KI-uh
Cayuse	ki-use
Umatilla	yoo-muh-TIL-uh

Umatilla County traces its creation in 1862 to the regional gold rushes, which spawned the river port of Umatilla City.

"14 miles to a rock in a Lard. Resembling a hat just below the rapid."

– CAPTAIN CLARK; Hat Rock retains its name from Lewis and Clark and sits prominently in Hat Rock State Park.

"...the pea farmers were praying for rain and at the same time the orchard owners were praying that it wouldn't rain."

– DESCRIPTION OF UMATILLA COUNTY'S HISTORY OF AGRICULTURE
Source: www.usgennet.org/usa/or/county/umatilla/pea_harvest.htm

"My family has lived and called Umatilla County home for six generations. My wife and I met at the University of Oregon, and 12 years after we graduated returned to the county, where I was raised, to in turn raise our family of six children. We have never regretted that decision. It is a very special place for us."

– BILL HANSELL, PENDLETON

OREGON AGRICULTURE; Winter Wheat field

"OREGON IS a magical place. From the sage brush scented plateaus to the hidden emerald treasures in the Blue Mountains, this is a state which takes your breath away. In my work I have had the pleasure of travelling all over the state and visiting every county. I have been asked many times where is the most beautiful part of the state. This is a question that can't be answered, for the truth of the matter, it is the place you are in at that moment. This sounds like a cliché, but Oregon is too magnificent to reduce to a single place, person or thing. I am grateful every day for the chance to see the breeze blow on a wheat field or the clouds flood the sky over one of our many mountain tops; it shapes our view of ourselves and our faith in the future. Oregon is more than one person can take in a single lifetime. That is why songs, poetry and art are so important to future generations; they serve as tastes of what is to come if you remain open to the experience that is Oregon. The only divide that exists in Oregon is the one between what you've seen and what you will never get to experience. As Oregonians, life is simply too short."

– STAN FOSTER, WESTON MOUNTAIN

PENDLETON ROUND-UP
86 Years of Western Tradition

RODEO FANS from around the world head to Northeastern Oregon in September for the Pendleton Round-up. The event draws 50,000 people to the area. It's the largest four-day rodeo in the country.

The event started as a 4th of July celebration in 1909, but moved to September the next year to accommodate local agricultural schedules. That first event included horse races, Native American feasts and war dances, greased pig contests, sack races, foot races, and fireworks.

Today calf roping, bronco riding, steer wrestling, barrel racing, bull riding, and wild cow milking are some of the activities included in this grand western tradition.

PENDLETON ROUND-UP
86 years of tradition

PENDLETON ROUND-UP
PENDLETON ROUND-UP
PENDLETON ROUND-UP
Let 'er Buck
PENDLETON
LETON-ROUND-UP
Let 'er Buck
PENDLETON
ROUND-UP

Union

COUNTY SEAT: Union County Commissioners, 1106 K Ave., La Grande 97850

PHONE: 541-963-1006

WEB: www.union-county.org

ESTABLISHED: Oct. 14, 1864

ELEV. AT LA GRANDE: 2,788'

AREA: 2,038 sq. mi.

AVERAGE TEMP.: Jan. 30.9°, July 70.4°

ANNUAL PRECIPITATION: 18.79"

ECONOMY: Agriculture, forest products, education, and government.

POINTS OF INTEREST: Meacham and Tollgate winter sports areas, Grande Ronde Valley, Eastern Oregon University (La Grande).

GEOGRAPHIC PRONUNCIATIONS	
Imbler	IM-bluhr
Elgin	EL-gin
Grande Ronde Valley	rawnd

"IT'S LATE October and after a long dry summer, I savor the smell and feel of moisture in the air. Clouds are dancing along the tops of the mountains in every direction. I've walked across the meadows to my favorite spot on the bank of the Powder River and have knelt to turn a few river rocks and admire the glittering chunks of granite on the shore. In spite of the crisp, clear air, the sun is warm on my back. I stand and follow the rippling water. To the west, the Elkhorn peaks of the Blue Mountains are lightly dusted with fresh snow. Below the snow line, the blazing orange of Tamarack trees shows their final burst of energy before they shed their needles and sleep for the winter. To the east, the tips of the Wallowas are already white and begin to blush as the day ages. On whispering wings, a pair of mallards flies by, and overhead a flock of Canada geese gently calls to each other. With every change of the seasons, I say to myself, 'this is my favorite time of year'...until the next one."

– JANET DODSON, LA GRANDE

GRANDE RONDE VALLEY FROM THE BLUE MOUNTAINS

*"This is a place—one of the few we have seen
in our journey so far—where a
farmer would delight himself to establish."*

———

JOHN C. FREMONT'S JOURNAL ENTRY OF
THE GRANDE RONDE VALLEY, OCTOBER 1843

Wallowa

COUNTY SEAT: Courthouse,
101 S River St., Enterprise 97828
PHONE: 541-426-4543, ext. 15
WEB: www.eoni.com/~mhayward/county
ESTABLISHED: Feb. 11, 1887
ELEV. AT ENTERPRISE: 3,757'
AREA: 3,153 sq. mi.
AVERAGE TEMP.: Jan. 24.2°, July 63.0°
ANNUAL PRECIPITATION: 13.08"

ECONOMY: Agriculture, art, livestock, forest products, and recreation.
POINTS OF INTEREST: Wallowa Lake, art galleries, Mt. Howard gondola, Eagle Cap Wilderness, Hells Canyon National Recreation Area.

GEOGRAPHIC PRONUNCIATIONS	
Imnaha River	IM-na-ha
Wallowa	wah-LAO-uh

Tucked away in the northeast corner of Oregon, small communities are surrounded by rugged mountains, deep canyons, plateaus, and rolling hills.

Source: www.wallowacountychamber.com/tourist.htm

Hells Canyon is one of the most imposing river gorges in the West. It is the deepest gorge in the United States. Below Hells Canyon Dam, the Snake River usually carries more water than the Colorado River through the Grand Canyon.

Wallowa County lies almost entirely in the Grande Ronde River Basin. Its small communities are surrounded by rugged mountains, deep canyons, plateaus and rolling hills. Wallowa County has 53 lakes and 3,100 streams, and its Indian name means "Land of the Winding Waters."

The gondola of the Wallowa Lake Tramway is a Swiss-made tram, and was constructed in 1970 as the steepest vertical lift for a four-passenger gondola in North America. In just under 15 minutes, you are taken from the bottom terminal at 4,450' up to 8,150' atop Mt. Howard. The highest point off the ground is 120 feet.

Sources: www.wallowacounty.org, www.wallowalaketramway.com

WALLOWA LAKE; Fall colored cottonwoods

WHAT MAKES LIVING IN WALLOWA COUNTY SPECIAL?

"After a life of unsettled wandering and traveling, I happened upon this exquisite corner of the earth and was finally...home. Words can't express the secure embrace of these Wallowa Mountains, the high prairies, the canyons, and the family of people who make their lives here."

– WENDY HANSEN, ENTERPRISE

"The main reason I like living in Wallowa County is something that can't be put into words."

– TIM PERALES, ENTERPRISE

"What I love about living in Wallowa County is how happy the people are in the spring!"

– SUSAN GILSTRAP, ENTERPRISE

"Oregon, like good music, permeates the soul, lifts the spirit, and swells the heart. Wallowa County holds the whole orchestra."

– SUSAN ROBERTS, MAYOR, ENTERPRISE, OREGON

HELLS CANYON
from Buckhorn Overlook, Wallowa County.

*"From the depths of the canyons, replete with cactus,
boulders, rushing rivers to the high mountains,
pristine with snow atop, wildflowers that come until
late in the summer, and the crown of sky and
spectacular sunsets—all of these things are inspiration
for my artistic bent. All of these things are a necessary
backdrop for what means so much to me—visual art."*

— E. SLINKER, ENTERPRISE

"AN INDIAN died in a Walla Walla hospital last Tuesday, and they brought him home to the Wallowas on Thursday. That night they held Washat services for him at the Wallowa Senior Center, and Friday he was buried in the Wallowa Cemetery. The casket was draped in an Indian blanket and an American flag. At the service, I looked around and I was proud of being there and proud of the other non-Indians who were there serving food and listening to the service and participating in their own ways. We were all part of the dream that this man had, his dream of a Nez Perce homecoming and a space for Indian and non-Indians of the Wallowas to come together and celebrate history and culture, the central and important things. And to remember the Presbyterian Cayuse chief who made a prayer ten or twelve years ago on Chief Joseph Days at the first Indian Friendship Feast that this would be a place where white and white, white and Indian, Indian and Indian buried old differences and healed old wounds."

— RICH WANDSCHNEIDER, ENTERPRISE

Wasco

COUNTY SEAT: Courthouse,
511 Washington St., The Dalles 97058
PHONE: 541-296-6159
EMAIL: wasco1@netcnct.net
ESTABLISHED: Jan. 11, 1854
ELEV. AT THE DALLES: 98'
AREA: 2,396 sq. mi.
AVERAGE TEMP.: Jan. 33.4°, July 73.1°
ANNUAL PRECIPITATION: 14.90"
ECONOMY: Agriculture, forest products,
manufacturing, electric power, aluminum,
and transportation.

POINTS OF INTEREST: The Dalles
Dam, Confederated Tribes of the
Warm Springs Reservation, Mt. Hood,
Columbia River Gorge Discovery
Center.

GEOGRAPHIC PRONUNCIATIONS	
Celilo	suh-LIE-lo
Dufur	DOO-fur
Maupin	MAW-pin
Mosier	MO-zhuhr
Tygh Valley	tie

The County originally comprised all the area of the Oregon
Territory between the Cascade Range and the Rocky Mountains,
the largest county in U.S. history. Successive takings for other
states and counties has reduced this area.
Source: Oregon Geographic Names

The Dalles was where pioneers loaded their wagons onto
rafts or barges and floated down the Columbia to the mouth of
the Willamette River, then upriver to Oregon City. The Barlow
Trail was constructed later to permit an overland crossing.

"...the scenery along I-84 changes from lush forests to rain-
starved mountains in about the time it takes to pop in a new CD."

Source: AAA VIA MAGAZINE, www.csaa.com

Wheat harvest, Wasco County

"FULL MOONLIGHT filtered softly through high, thin clouds. Echoes of a swift river splashing over rocks came gurgling from the right. Sagebrush cast eerie shadows, warning one to walk carefully. A gentle breeze carried the pungent odor of a dying campfire. The cabin and its occupants slumbered.

Three a.m. on a crisp, cold night along the Deschutes brought a shiver, but the soul was at peace."

– BILL SNOUFFER, PORTLAND

Washington

COUNTY SEAT: Public Services Bldg., 155 N 1st Ave., Hillsboro 97124-3072

PHONE: 503-846-8741

WEB: www.co.washington.or.us

ESTABLISHED: July 5, 1843

ELEV. AT HILLSBORO: 196'

AREA: 727 sq. mi.

AVERAGE TEMP.: Jan. 39.9°, July 66.6°

ANNUAL PRECIPITATION: 37.71"

ECONOMY: Agriculture, horticulture, forest products, food processing, electronics, sports equipment, and apparel.

POINTS OF INTEREST: Tualatin Valley orchards and vineyards, high tech.

GEOGRAPHIC PRONUNCIATIONS	
Aloha	uh-LO-a
Tualatin	too-WAHL-uh-tin
Helvetia	hel-VAY-shah

Often referred to as the "Silicon Forest" for its continuing growth in the area of high technology, Washington County is home to electronics leaders such as Intel and Tektronix, and is World Headquarters for Nike, Inc. It is the second largest and fastest growing county in Oregon, with approximately 445,342 citizens. Washington County is 727 square miles.

With comparisons to the world's finest climates and best soils, Washington County is home to many of Oregon's premier wineries. But it takes more than quality grapes to produce award-winning wines. It takes vintners who love the art of winemaking. Washington County wineries are often small and family-owned, passing through generations of fathers and sons, mothers and daughters. The wineries are nestled in the foothills with rows of vines as far as you can see, tended by hands devoted to the art. It is that extra touch that helps these wineries overflow with charm and legend.

Source: www.wcva.org

Hillsboro, Oregon, the county seat, is home to SOLV's statewide headquarters office.

Late afternoon sun over fields of grasses

"OREGON NEVER ceases to amaze me—not just its beauty but its people and the soft spot they carry in their heart for her. I have traveled all over the west, and when I explain to others how we love and protect this wonderfully diverse place and go to great pains to take care of her, they are always envious. I am just as proud to be an Oregonian as I am to be an American."

– PEGGY DAY, HILLSBORO

Wheeler

COUNTY SEAT: Wheeler County,
701 Adams St., PO Box 327,
Fossil 97830
PHONE: 541-763-2400
ESTABLISHED: Feb. 17, 1899
ELEV. AT FOSSIL: 2,654'
AREA: 1,713 sq. mi.
AVERAGE TEMP.: Jan. 35°, July 66°

ANNUAL PRECIPITATION: 14.66"
ECONOMY: Livestock and tourism.
POINTS OF INTEREST: Painted Hills,
John Day Fossil Beds, John Day River.

GEOGRAPHIC PRONUNCIATIONS	
Kinzua	kin-ZOO-a

Wheeler County is as rugged and uneven as any Oregon county, with the terrain varying widely from sagebrush, juniper, and rim rock to stands of pine and fir. Portions of two national forests lie within its boundaries with forestlands covering nearly one-third of the county. The area is probably best known as one of the most outstanding depositories of prehistoric fossils on the North American continent.

"THE HIGH desert after an early fall thunderstorm has an aroma that is near ecstasy. The skies so clear that a 90-mile view is routine. Sage, grass, and water all combine into an experience to be savored. The best of all is the high open forest of Eastern Oregon on a brisk fall morning after a rain the night before. The combination of juniper, sage, pine, and fir is simply incredible. The quiet, peaceful surroundings totally encompass one to the point that you truly feel as though you are together, harmonious with nature at last."

– THOMAS CUTSFORTH, FOSSIL

SHEEP ROCK UNIT
John Day Fossil Beds National Monument

Yamhill

COUNTY SEAT: Courthouse,
535 NE 5th St., McMinnville 97128
PHONE: 503-434-7518
WEB: www.co.yamhill.or.us
ESTABLISHED: July 5, 1843
ELEV. AT MCMINNVILLE: 157'
AREA: 718 sq. mi.
AVERAGE TEMP.: Jan. 39.0°, July 65.0°
ANNUAL PRECIPITATION: 43.6"
ECONOMY: Agriculture, wine production, steel manufacturing, forest products, dental instruments, and aircraft servicing.

POINTS OF INTEREST: Linfield College, George Fox University, Herbert Hoover House, military blockhouse, Yamhill County Historical Museum, Wheatland Ferry, Captain Michael Smith Evergreen Aviation Educational Center, Rogers Landing.

GEOGRAPHIC PRONUNCIATIONS	
Willamina	will-a-MY-na
Wapato	WAH-pah-to
Chehalem	shuh-HAIL-em

"Founded in 1843 as one of four original Oregon Counties, Yamhill County lies in the northern end of the Willamette Valley. Its 718 square miles contain lush farmland, fine wineries, the world famous 'Spruce Goose', and a historical heritage unsurpassed in Oregon."

Source: www.co.yamhill.or.us

By the 1860s nearly all of the tillable farmland in the county had been claimed, purchased, or homesteaded. Farming became the primary endeavor of our settlers, especially after most of the fathers and brothers returned from the goldfields.

AUTUMNAL VINEYARDS IN YAMHILL COUNTY
Oregon's combination of northern latitude, occasional marine breezes, and
long hours of sunshine create warm summer days and a gently cooling autumn.
Her noble grape varieties ripen gradually under moderate temperatures.
Source: www.oregonwine.org

Yamhill County, where the rolling hills are covered with row upon
row of lush grape vines, is home to the largest concentration of
wineries and vineyards in the state of Oregon. Fifty-five wineries
lie scattered throughout the county and produce the greatest
number of award-winning wines in the state. Many Yamhill
County wineries are achieving national and international promi-
nence with their award-winning wines, notably Pinot Noir, the
flagship wine of Oregon, as well as Pinot Gris.

Sources: www.co.yamhill.or.us, www.oregonwine.org, and www.winesnw.com

"Joanne and I have lived here since 1979. We expect this poem is 100+ years old and feel it is valid today. Living on the 'edge' of the valley has its advantages and rewards!"

– JOHN & JOANNE PITHDO, YAMHILL

OLD YAMHILL

Fairest County in the West
Loved by all of us the best
In the state where nature all her wealth unfurled,
Uncle Samie's "Garden Spot"
Where its neither cold nor hot
Against the world.

Chorus:
Old Yamhill, our fav'rite county
Old Yamhill we sing of thee.
Fertile fields with bumper crops
Fruit and nuts and garden plots
Logs and lumber and outstanding Industry.

Towns where one may shop with ease,
Schools and colleges that please,
Clubs and churches and the best society.
Friends and neighbors, who are true
And always kind to you
It's the finest kind of place to live, you see

– AUTHOR UNKNOWN

Icicles cling to eaves of log cabin.

SOLV

WANT TO get involved with keeping Oregon the special place it is? SOLV offers a variety of volunteer programs that do just that. For more information, visit www.solv.org or call 800-333-SOLV.

SIGNATURE EVENTS

GREAT OREGON BEACH CLEANUPS—*Spring & Fall*
The entire Oregon coastline is cleaned of litter and marine debris, returning it to its pristine condition for visitors and wildlife. Coordinated with Oregon Parks & Recreation Department.

SOLV IT—*Spring*
One of the largest Earth Day activities in the nation. Illegal dumpsite cleanups and neighborhood enhancement projects are undertaken throughout Northwest Oregon.

INTEL-SOLV WASHINGTON COUNTY CLEAN AND GREEN PROJECT—*Fall*
Cleanup and enhancement of neighborhoods, parks, and rights-of-way plus maintenance of senior and disabled citizen homes and social service properties.

WATERWAY PROGRAMS

DOWN BY THE RIVERSIDE—*Spring*
Cleanup and enhancement projects on waterside public spaces. Parks, marinas, and natural areas benefit.

OREGON ADOPT-A-RIVER—*Year Round*
Volunteers select two-mile segments of waterways to keep clean of litter and debris. Provided in partnership with the Oregon State Marine Board.

TEAM UP FOR WATERSHED HEALTH—*Year Round*
A coalition of government, businesses, non-profit organizations, and citizen volunteers, working on restoration projects in the lower Willamette watershed. SOLV matches volunteers and resources with each site.

COMMUNITY RESOURCES

PROJECT OREGON—*Year Round*

Provides technical and financial assistance, and free materials to communities throughout Oregon for cleanup, beautification, and enhancement projects. Kicked off in May by Oregon's governor on the steps of the capitol.

K-12 YOUTH EDUCATION PROGRAMS—*Year Round*

Service-learning curriculum and project planning guides aligned to state academic benchmarks and standards, for classroom use by Oregon K-12 teachers. Some education programs include technical and financial assistance for project implementation.

N/NE COMMUNITY ACTION PROGRAM—*Year Round*

A partnership with Tri-Met to mobilize North/Northeast Portland residents in ongoing cleanup and enhancement projects and promote the Adopt-A-Stop program.

SOLV-U.S. BANK BEST OF OREGON PROGRAM—*October–September*

A partnership that supports rural Oregon communities with intensive staff support, project funds, volunteer training, and planning assistance. Best of Oregon communities to date include Aurora, Banks, Dayton, Estacada, Garibaldi, Molalla, Nehalem, St. Paul, Tillamook, Vernonia, and Yamhill.

VOLUNTEER ACTION TRAINING—*Varies*

A full-day workshop that trains Oregonians to coordinate volunteer cleanup and enhancement projects throughout the state. Call for list of dates and locations.

"OREGON NEEDS to be preserved not only for Oregonians and the people of this nation, but as a model for the rest of the world. Although much work has yet to be done, Oregon has continually taken pride in being at the forefront of environmental conservation and preservation. As the rest of the world sees Oregonians able to mix economic prosperity with conservation, they will be encouraged to balance their communities, cities, and countries in a healthier manner. In my experience, most out-of-state visitors I've ever talked to feel there is something unique about the land and the people that inhabit Oregon. There is a friendliness in manner that comes directly from a people proud of where they live and the steps they've taken to keep it that way. This is what Oregon is about, and we should share it with others so they too can create an environment of which they are protective and proud.

When away from Oregon, I miss mostly the wide open spaces and the people that are working to preserve them."

— BOONE JOHNSON, PORTLAND

◄ CANOLA FIELD IN THE ROGUE RIVER VALLEY

INDEX

To submit corrections, ideas, or content for
future editions of the *Oregon Owner's Manual*,
write to info@solv.org, or:

SOLV

P.O. Box 1235

Hillsboro, OR 97123